D1413389

THE PRESS IN NIGERIA

Recent Titles in
African Special Bibliographic Series

American-Southern African Relations: Bibliographic Essays
Mohamed A. El-Khawas and Francis A. Kornegay, Jr.

A Short Guide to the Study of Ethiopia: A General Bibliography
Alula Hidaru and Dessalegn Rahmato

Afro-Americans and Africa: Black Nationalism at the Crossroads
William B. Helmreich

Somalia: A Bibliographical Survey
Mohamed Khalief Salad

Ethiopian Perspectives: A Bibliographical Guide to the History of Ethiopia
Clifton F. Brown

A Bibliography of African Ecology: A Geographically and Topically Classified
List of Books and Articles
Dilwyn J. Rogers, compiler

Demography, Urbanization, and Spatial Planning in Kenya: A Bibliographical Survey
Robert A. Obudho

Population, Urbanization, and Rural Settlement in Ghana: A Bibliographic Survey
Joseph A. Sarfoh, compiler

African Women: A General Bibliography, 1976-1985
Davis A. Bullwinkle, compiler

Women of Northern, Western, and Central Africa: A Bibliography, 1976-1985
Davis A. Bullwinkle, compiler

Women of Eastern and Southern Africa: A Bibliography, 1976-1985
Davis A. Bullwinkle, compiler

THE PRESS IN NIGERIA
An Annotated Bibliography

Compiled by
Chris W. Ogbondah

Foreword by
Joseph P. McKerns

African Special Bibliographic Series, Number 12

GREENWOOD PRESS
New York • Westport, Connecticut • London

Library of Congress Cataloging-in-Publication Data

Ogbondah, Chris W.
    The press in Nigeria : an annotated bibliography / compiled by
Chris W. Ogbondah.
        p.   cm.—(African special bibliographic series, ISSN
0749-2308 ; no. 12)
    Includes index.
    ISBN 0-313-26521-6 (lib. bdg. : alk. paper)
    1. Press—Nigeria—Bibliography. I. Title. II. Series.
Z6940.034 1990
[PN5499.N5]
016.079′669—dc20   90-3676

British Library Cataloguing in Publication Data is available.

Library of Congress Catalog Card Number: 90-3676
ISBN: 0-313-26521-6
ISSN: 0749-2308

First published in 1990

Greenwood Press, 88 Post Road West, Westport, CT 06881
An imprint of Greenwood Publishing Group, Inc.

Printed in the United States of America

The paper used in this book complies with the
Permanent Paper Standard issued by the National
Information Standards Organization (Z39.48-1984).

10 9 8 7 6 5 4 3 2 1

8-21-90

Dedicated to Wobo and Gaga

Contents

Foreword *by Joseph P. McKerns*   ix

Introduction   xi

An Annotated Bibliography   1

Index   113

Foreword

That mass communication is central to the life of any
modern nation is a point that ceased to be debatable a
long time ago. When we study a nation's media system,
its current status and its past, it is as if we are
examining the development and functioning of that
nation's central nervous system. Just as a body can
not maintain itself without a workable mass media
system for the communication of vital, and even not-so-
vital, information, whether business, political,
social, cultural institutional, or instructional.

   Nigeria is a key nation among the emerging nations
of Africa. This bibliography on its mass media should
be warmly welcomed and applauded by scholars in the
fields of African Studies and International
Communications, as well as other related fields. It is
a pleasure to be able to play even this minor role in a
work that, I believe, will be considered a major
contribution to the literature of scholarship on the
subject.

   Little did I realize that when Professor Ogbondah,
then my doctoral student, completed an independent
study in media history under my supervision at Southern
Illinois University at Carbondale that it would blossom
as a book-length bibliography several years later.
While I may have helped plant the seed of this volume
by suggesting that an annotated bibliography on the
Nigeria press and its history would make a worthy
independent study project, I was only trying to do my
job as would any graduate faculty member. Professor
Ogbondah was the gardener who nurtured the seed and

made it blossom into this worthy work.

Professor Ogbondah has given to the field of Nigerian media studies what the benchmark works of Warren Price and Calder Pickett, The Literature of Journalism[1] and An Annotated Journalism Bibliography, 1958-1968,[2] gave to the field of American media studies. We all are enriched by it.

Joseph P. McKerns, Ph.D.
School of Journalism
Ohio State University

Notes

[1] Warren C. Price, The Literature of Journalism: An Annotated Bibliography (Minneapolis: University of Minnesota Press, 1959).

[2] Warren C. Price and Calder Pickett, An Annotated Journalism Bibliography, 1958-1968 (Minneapolis: University of Minnesota Press, 1970).

Introduction

The history of mass communication in Nigeria predates
the history of the first printed newspaper, <u>Iwe Irohin</u>,
which was established in 1859. Yet interest in
research publications in Nigerian journalism or the
broad field of mass communication did not begin until
at about the close of the 1950's and early 1960's. It
was during that period that the pioneer works of
Aloba,[1] Oton,[2] Coleman,[3] Mackintosh,[4] Azikiwe[5] and
Ainslie[6] were published. The toddling efforts of the
late 1950's came of age in the 1970's (when new social
and economic conditions by way of oil boom opened
unprecedented opportunities in higher education and
academe in Nigeria) and matured in the 1980's.

Today, Nigeria has nineteen communication and
quasi-communication training programs offering
qualifications that range from certificates to Ordinary
National and Higher National Diplomas to Bachelors and
Masters degrees [7] and student as well as faculty
research publications have increased quantitatively and
qualitatively. Beyond the shores of Nigeria,
especially in the United States and Great Britain,
several universities and research institutions and
agencies have turned out handsome volumes of research
works on Nigerian press. In the United States
especially almost all institutions offering graduate
programs in mass communication or journalism have
turned out masters or doctoral dissertations on
Nigerian press including print journalism,
broadcasting, film, cinematography and traditional
(folk) media.

A fairly commendable volume of scholarly works on
the press has also been published in books and academic
and professional journals. In addition, a handsome
quantity of unpublished papers on the press has been

presented at institutional, regional, national and
international academic platforms (especially in
Nigeria, United States and Britain).

One may wonder where these works may be found and
how they can be categorized. Regrettably enough,
however, there is no single book of annotated
bibliography where all these works may be found, even
though a suggestion has been made at least once for the
need for a single body of literature of what has been
written and published on Africa's most powerful and
vigorous press.

In an article in the <u>Gazette</u>, Ogbondah,[8] deplored
the absence of an annotated bibliography on the
Nigerian press. A casual remark on the importance of
such a book was also made by Ansah.[9] Perhaps, the
first known attempt in meeting this need was made by
Ogbondah.[10] Even that attempt was severely limited in
scope and depth. The works covered in that attempt
were presented in a bibliographical essay, covering
only a minuscule of what has been written or published
on press freedom, censorship, history and politics.
Thus, several areas of the press were wittingly or
unwittingly left out in that work which is, however,
worthy because of its pioneering effort. The author
himself recognized this limitation when he said: "This
paper does not present all the major works on Nigerian
press. . . . These include among others, works on
broadcasting."[11]

Attempts made to present some of the published
works in an annotated bibliography include a 1983
effort by the same author which listed a skeletal 173
items;[12] and a 1974 publication of 458 items of
annotated (sometimes unannotated) bibliography of
African broadcasting by Sydney Head (which included
very few items on Nigeria).[13] Like the work mentioned
before it, Sydney Head's work is limited for its
incomprehensive form. William Hachten in an annotated
bibliography of African press, listed probably fewer
items than Sydney Head on Nigeria. Though commendable
it is, professor Hachten's work suffers from the same
limitation found in Ogbondah and Head.

The present work is being undertaken in an attempt
to meet a demand for an annotated bibliography of
Nigerian press. The importance of a book of this
nature has been well stated by Woseley and Wolseley,[14]
Price and Pickett,[15] as well as by professors Edwin
Emery and Frank Mott in their annotated bibliographies
of American press.

But suffice it to add that this book will
specially make literature search on Nigerian press
easier for scholars of International Communication in
general and Nigerian press in particular. Hitherto,
researchers on Nigerian press must painfully search

through several dry sources for what has been written or published about the press. Sometimes they search in vain and at other times, they are lucky to come across items scattered here and there like the seeds of oil bean trees of tropical Nigeria. This book is a pioneer effort to alleviate some of the pains associated with research on Nigerian press.

No single work of science stands independent of other works. Each piece serves as a building block for subsequent works, according to Lowery and Defleur in their book, <u>Milestones in Mass Communication Research</u>.[16] Any socially redeeming value of this work, among other things, is that it brings together information on building blocks for subsequent works on Nigerian press.

This book steers a pioneering academic exercise in bibliographical compilation on Nigerian mass communication; and it is hoped that in the future, such exercises should be geared toward compiling bibliographies on specialized areas of mass communication such as print journalism, public relations, advertising, broadcasting, etc.

The works listed in this book are scholarly journal articles, books, conference papers and reports on Nigerian mass communication. An annotation of each work is made by pointing out its main point, its main thesis, summary, conclusion or research questions. The items are listed in alphabetic order of the authors' last names and where they can be found are mentioned along with the dates of publication or presentation. Articles and reports lacking authors' names are entered as "ANON" (anonymous).

Some of the items are not in the classical sense, formal academic research endeavors. They are articles or essays written by professional media practitioners and are therefore useful for inclusion in this book for what media scholars, theorists, law makers and students may learn of the experiences of practitioners in the field. Such items have also been included because of the reputation of the sources in which they were published.

This book is not meant to be, nor should it be understood to be comprehensive on the subject the author treats. What is seen in this first edition is the tip of the iceberg. Therefore, the author does not claim finality in the treatment of the subject. Many items could not be included because the author did not reach or verify them. Several works published in Nigeria or conducted in Nigerian universities could not be reached for inclusion in this edition. It is hoped that the second edition will be more comprehensive and include such works.

Another problem the author faces which is perhaps,

the dilemma of most bibliographers who annotate entries is that of deciding when to make a more detailed entry and when to present lesser details. However, detailed comments have been made when the works being annotated contain several themes, conclusions, objectives or research questions. Fewer comments are made when the works' major theses are simple to be presented in a few words.

Because the author has utilized straight alphabetical listing of these works, it is advised that persons using this book depend more on the cross-references (index) at the end for specific topics or categories. The author considers this method more useful in assisting readers to find what they want rather than using subject categorization in the main text since some of the works overlap one another.

The author wishes to thank Joseph P. McKerns at the School of Journalism at Ohio State University for his immeasurable support, assistance and advice in compiling this bibliography. My thanks also go to friends whose endearing encouragement and moral support have helped me put this work together. Among them are Gary Whitby, Momo Rogers, Pita Agbese, Ben Wodi and Rev. George Howard, Sr. Finally, I express my gratitude to Greenwood Press for issuing this book. I have no shadow of doubts in mind that under its publisher, this book will gain wide circulation.

The author welcomes suggestions for additions, changes or corrections of errors of omission or commission that might be found in this first edition. Such suggestions or comments may be sent to the author at the Department of English Language and Literature, University of Northern Iowa, Cedar Falls, Iowa 50613.

Notes

[1] Abiodun Aloba, "Journalism in Africa: I. Nigeria," Gazette, vol. 5, no. 2, 1959, pp. 245-248; see also Gazette, vol. 5, no. 3, 1959, pp. 317-321; Gazette, vol. 5, no. 4, 1959, pp. 409-412.

[2] Esuakema U. Oton, "Developments in Nigerian Journalism," Journalism Quarterly, vol. 35, 1958, pp. 72-80.

[3] James S. Coleman, Nationalism in Nigeria, Ph.D dissertation, Harvard University, 1953; see also James Coleman, Nigeria: Background to Nationalism, Berkeley, California: University of California Press, 1958.

[4] John P. Mackintosh, Nigerian Government and Politics: Prelude to the Revolution. Evanston, Illinois: Northwestern University Press, 1966.

[5] Nnamdi Azikiwe, "Journalism in West Africa," West African Pilot (Nigeria), May 18 - June 13, 1945.

[6] Rosalynde Ainslie, The Press in Africa: Communications Past and Present. New York: Walker and Company, 1966.

[7] Ikechukwu E. Nwosu, "Mass Media Discipline and Control in Contemporary Nigeria: A Contextual Critical Analysis," Gazette, vol. 39, no. 1, 1987, pp. 17-29.

[8] Chris W. Ogbondah, "Nigerian Journalism: A Bibliographical Essay," Gazette, vol. 36, 1985, pp. 175-191.

[9] See P.A.V. Ansah's book review in Journal of Communication, vol. 36, no. 2, 1986, pp. 162-164.

[10] Chris W. Ogbondah, Ibid.

[11] Ibid.

[12] Chris W. Ogbondah, "A Selected Bibliography of Nigerian Press," School at Journalism, Southern Illinois University of Carbondale, 1983.

[13] Sydney W. Head & Lois Beck. Bibliography of African Broadcasting: An Annotated Guide, Philadelphia: School of Communications and Theater, Temple University, 1974.

[14] Roland E. Woseley and Isabel Wolseley. The Journalist's Bookshelf: An Annotated and Selected Bibliography of United States Print Journalism. Indianapolis, Indiana: R. J. Berg & Company Publishers, Inc., 1986.

[15] Warren C. Price and Calder M. Pickett, An Annotated Journalism Bibliography 1958-1968. Minneapolis: University of Minnesota Press, 1970.

[16] Shearon Lowery & Melvin L. DeFleur. Milestones in Mass Communication Research: Media Effects. New York: Longman, 1983.

An Annotated Bibliography

1. ABOABA, Doyinsola A. "A Case Study of Radio
Nigeria." M.A. thesis, University of Wisconsin, 1972.
This thesis provides a philosophical and historical
overview of radio broadcasting in Nigeria. It analyzes
the suitability of radio broadcasting to national
development as well as the contribution of the medium
in that respect. An attempt is also made to sketch the
history of the industry.

2. ABOABA, Doyinsola A. The Nigerian Press Under
Military Rule. Ph.D dissertation, State University of
New York at Buffalo, 1979.
What are the limits of press transformations which
military rule can bring about in West Africa? This is
the question raised in this study. Nigeria, which was
under military rule when this study was undertaken, is
used as a case study. The study shows that the
interrelationship between the military government and
the press is not monolithic or simple. The greatest
source of conflict between the military and the press
is the authoritarian nature of the military which
conflicts with press operation that is based on the
idea of "open forum of debate."

3. ABORISADE, Adebisi A. The International News
"Imbalance": A Nigerian Case Study. Ph.D dissertation,
University of Minnesota, 1980.
This dissertation investigates the extent to which
Nigerians are being exposed to foreign news in terms
of: I) the kinds of information the Nigerian press
transmits and the relative attention the press pays to
events abroad; 2) the favorable or unfavorable images
of countries this information is likely to convey to
readers; and 3) the attitudes of Nigerian journalists
on the issue of "imbalance" in international news flow.
Among other things, the study shows that Nigerian
journalists perceive their readers as
"internationalists" who are very keen about events in
other countries.

4. ACKER, Vincent. "La Presse au Nigeria et au Ghana"
The Press in Nigeria and Ghana. Rev. Francaise
d'Etudes Pol. Africanes, no. 84, 1972, pp. 72-94.
An examination of the large number of publications in
Nigeria and Ghana and the reasons behind their success,
such as the effects of British liberalism and the
influence of large populations of African American
immigrants. Also views problems of national social and
economic development, despite great progress in the
media.

5.   ADEGBUYI, Akin.   "Future of Public Service
Broadcasting in Nigeria," Combroad, no. 66, 1985, pp.
18-23.
A look at Nigeria's public service broadcasting, with
special reference to its objectives, constituent
public, its future and problems, especially inadequate
funding. The main conclusion is that the future of
public service broadcasting in Nigeria, and indeed in
other developing countries of the Commonwealth, will
continue to be directly related to political and
cultural developments, while the aspirations, needs and
requirements of the people will always determine which
way public service broadcasting should go.

6.   ADEJUMOBI, Jonathan A.   "The Development of Radio
Broadcasting in Nigeria, West Africa." M.A.   thesis,
North Texas State University, 1974.
This study examines the history of radio broadcasting
as well as the industry's structure as of 1974.   The
main conclusion is that the structure of Nigerian radio
is a direct product of the peculiar history of the
country as a former British colony.   The author
contends that little can be done to solve the problems
of Nigerian radio unless the problems of Nigeria are
first solved.

7.   ADELEYE, Samuel A.   "The Mass Media in an Emerging
Democracy: Determining Nigerian Students' Attitudes
Toward Freedom of the Press in Nigeria," M.A. thesis,
Oklahoma State University, 1981.
An examination of attitudes of Nigerian university
students toward government restrictions on the Nigerian
press.   Samples of students from Oklahoma State
University and University of Ibadan (Nigeria) were used
in the study.   Results show that Nigerian students at
Oklahoma State University were more favorable toward
freedom of the press in Nigeria than their Nigerian
counterparts.   Nigerian students from the northern
states of the country were less favorable to press
freedom than their southern states counterparts.
Overall, however, Nigerian Students at home and abroad
tend to be against government restrictions on the
press.

8.   ADENLE, Shola.   "The Press and the Election,"
Nigerian Opinion," vol. 1, no. 1, 1965, pp. 11-12.
The author's main contention is that if the press of a
nation reflects the state of that nation's society,
Nigerian newspapers gave a very puzzling, piece-meal
reflections during the elections in the First Republic.
During the election, the most detailed news came to the
Nigerian public from the BBC, a foreign broadcasting

service. The author argues that if government-owned
newspapers which are supported with the taxpayer's
money cannot provide the most complete news coverage
for the nation, the nation might as well find a better
way to spend millions of taxpayers' money.

9. ADUROJA, Elias I. "Broadcasting in Nigeria -- A
Survey of Radio, Television and Film Industry," M.S.
thesis, Oklahoma State University, 1979.
An examination of the history, operations,
organizational structure and the role of Nigerian
broadcasting industry in national government. Aspects
of press freedom and government control of the industry
are mentioned. The main conclusion is that government
is becoming more and more involved in ownership and
control of the media. Some recommendations for
improving performance are made.

10. African Council on Communication Education.
Africa Speaks, America Responds. Washington, D.C.:
African Council on Communication Education Dialogue,
1979.
Defines a number of African communication priorities
and needs that challenge the United States and other
Western nations to provide a coordinated response to
the major changes in the field of cooperative
communication assistance to meet Africa's development
objectives. Training and education is particularly
discussed, and the views of two Nigerian mass
communication professors -- Sylvanus Ekwelie and Alfred
Opubor -- are well stated in the thirty-eight-page
report.

11. AGBA, Paul C. A Configurational analysis of the
Diffusion Models and Media Strategies Used in the
"Operation Feed the Nation" (OFN) Campaign in Nigeria
1976-1979. Ph.D dissertation, Indiana University,
1980.
Examines the compatibility and the effectiveness of the
diffusion models and media strategies used during the
Operation Feed the nation (OFN) campaign. The study
concludes that Nigerian policy makers and planners did
an excellent job of conceptualizing and planning the
campaign, accommodating among their concerns the use of
appropriate diffusion models and media strategies,
institution building and incentive management,
provision of knowledge and material inputs as well as
local participation.

12. AGBESE, Pita O. "State, Media and the Imperatives
of Repression: An Analysis of the Ban on Newswatch."

Paper Presented at the eleventh Third World Studies
Conference, Omaha, Nebraska, October 19-23, 1988.
An analytical essay on the six-month proscription of
the Newswatch magazine by the Ibrahim Babangida
military government. The author describes the
political events that precipitated the proscription
order, and explains far more than the government did,
why the news magazine was banned. How the Nigerian
public reacted to the ban of the Newswatch is also
described.

13. AGBOAYE, Ehikioya. "Nigerian Military Government
and Press Freedom, 1966-1979." M.A. thesis, North
Texas State University, 1984.
Did the activities of the military government violate
press freedom rights between 1966-1979? Were there
prior restraints on the press, post-publication
censorship and penalization? These were the major
questions addressed. The study shows that the military
violated some aspects of press freedom, but in most
cases, journalists were free to criticize government
activities. A major conclusion is that the judiciary
prevented the military from arbitrarily using its
powers to clamp down on the press.

14. AINSLIE, Rosalynde. The Press in Africa:
Communications Past and Present. New York: Walker and
Company, 1966.
An overview of the African press. An attempt is made
to chart the path of the history and development of the
press in West Africa, especially Nigeria. Statistical
information on the Nigerian media is given.

15. AKAGHA, Kevin C. A New World Information and
Communication Order: A Nigerian Response. Ph.D.
dissertation, University of Minnesota, 1984.
This study is mainly concerned with the Third World
call for a New World Information and Communication
Order, and Nigeria's response to it -- which is the
formation of the News Agency of Nigeria (NAN). The
study also examines the origin, structure, operations
and the sociopolitical role of the agency as well as
the social characteristics of its journalists, the
relationship between the agency and other national news
agencies. A composite profile of the agency's news
personnel is given: mostly male, professionally
oriented, well-paid, relatively young and well educated
but inexperienced journalists.

16. AKINFELEYE, Afolabi R. "Pre - and Post-
Independence Nigerian Journalism: (1859-1973)." M.A.
thesis, University of Missouri, 1974.

An Annotated Bibliography

This study's focus is on mass media development,
source, infrastructure, contents, use or uses and mass
media impact on the Nigerian people. The author has
made some effort to trace the history of the print and
electronic media. An examination of different types of
media ownership has been made. The study concludes
that the early Nigerian press was more outspoken,
politicized, diverse and competitive than the press of
later years, especially during the military rule.

17. AKINRINADE, Olusoji O. "Ownership Control v.
Editorial Content: A Study of Nigerian Daily Times."
M.A. thesis, University of Georgia, 1979.
Has the federal government ownership of sixty percent
equity shares in the Daily Times and total ownership of
the New Nigerian influenced the editorial contents of
both papers? No! The federal government does not
dictate the editorial content of both papers. The
Federal Military Government -- as of 1977 -- was more
benevolent toward the press than previous
administrations, and Nigerian press continued to retain
its freedom, despite military rule.

18. AKINTAYO, Olusola, "School Broadcasting in
Nigeria," Combroad, July-September, 1974, pp. 34-37.
This is one of the many informative articles on
educational broadcasting written by Nigerian
Broadcasting Corporation (NBC) staff.

19. AKPAN, Emmanuel D. A. "A Prospective Role For
Rural Adult Television in Nigeria." M.A. thesis,
California State University, San Francisco, 1970.
Examines the prospects of rural adult television
particularly in an educational capacity.

20. AKPAN, Emmanuel D. News Photos and Stories:
Men's and Women's Roles in Two Nigerian Newspapers.
Ph.D dissertation, The Ohio State University, 1979.
This study is an attempt to obtain a picture of how
Nigerian women are presented in the Daily Times and New
Nigerian. It examines the roles women are perceived by
the press to play in Nigeria's social system, by
comparing their roles in news stories and pictures with
those of men in the two newspapers. Nigerian women are
minorities in their national press. Both papers gave
significantly more attention to men than women in their
news stories and pictures.

21. AKWULE, Raymond U. Telecommunications in West
Africa: An Analysis of Selected Diplomatic Elite
Perceptions of Regional Cooperation in the Field of

7

<u>Telecommunications Within the Economic Community of
West African States (ECOWAS)</u>.
An attempt to gain insight to the problems and
prospects of regional cooperation in the field of
telecommunications within the Economic Community of
West African States (ECOWAS). Nigeria is an
influential, powerful member of the community. The
study concludes that the most important consideration
in multinational telecommunications cooperation in West
Africa is not economic but political. Some policy
recommendations are made.

22. ALABI, Aremu. "Tap of High Authority," <u>IPI
Report</u>, vol. 22, no. 2, 1973, pp. 1, 3, 4.
This article describes some of the repressive actions
of the military government against journalists.
Special focus is made on an airport incident involving
a <u>Nigerian Tribune</u> reporter denied audience with
visiting president Leopold Senghor of Senegal during a
press conference in Lagos.

23. ALABI, Stephen A. "Content Analysis of Three
English-Language African Newspapers." M.S. thesis,
Ohio University, 1982.
Is the quality of news flowing into the African press
from foreign news agencies different from that of
domestic news and news from African news agencies?
This is the primary research question addressed in this
study, using the <u>Daily Times</u> of Nigeria, the <u>Rand Daily
Mail</u> of South Africa and the <u>Daily Nation</u> of Kenya.
Among other things, the study concludes that foreign
news stories vary in style in much the same way as
domestic stories, and the topic of the news story,
rather than the places determine the style.

24. ALALADE, Bode. "Educational Television in
Nigeria," <u>Combroad</u>, no. 61, 1983, pp. 5-10.
Author looks at educational television broadcasting
with special mention of some of its problems, including
the most serious, lack of funds. The main conclusion
is that in order to achieve high quality educational
television program in Nigeria, support must come from
teachers, the public and government.

25. ALALI, Andy O. <u>Nigerian Participation in
INTELSAT: An Analysis of Communication Development</u>.
Ph.D dissertation, Howard University, 1985.
This study evaluates Nigeria's participation in the
International Telecommunication Satellite Organization
(INTELSAT), and argues that as the giant of the African
region, Nigeria, through its development program
affects the development of other African countries.

The study suggests that Nigeria develops a national
scientific information bank, restructure its national
development plan to include the masses in the decision-
making process, and emphasize the complex interactions
that exist in the society.

26.   ALALI, Andy O.   "Multilingual Radio Broadcasting
in Nigeria," Combroad, no. 75, 1987, pp. 22-24.
Author examines the role of multi-lingual radio
broadcasting in maintaining or sustaining collective
identities in Nigeria's pluralistic society. The main
conclusion is that by allowing cultural participation,
the Nigerian multi-lingual radio broadcasting performs
a unifying function in a manner whereby programs are
able to translate other ethnic and cultural
complexities otherwise unfamiliar to each ethnic group.

27.   ALBRIGHT, James M.   "The Problems of Distributing
Books in Burma, Nigeria and Mexico." M.S. thesis,
Syracuse university, 1964.
An analysis of the problems of book distribution in
three developing countries, including Nigeria.
Recommendations are outlined for creating more useful
book distribution systems in those countries.

28.   ALI, Biu A.   A Comparative Analysis of Mass Media
Uses and Gratifications Among Three Ethnic Groups in
Nigeria.   Ph.D dissertation, Ohio University, 1980.
This study examines media behavior among the major
ethnic groups - the Hausa, Yoruba and Ibo - with the
aim of measuring the influence of selected socio-
economic variables on media uses and gratifications.
Education is found to be the most important predictor
of media uses and number of gratifications sought. The
Hausa's patterns of media uses and gratifications are
strikingly different from those of Yoruba and Ibo.
Some of the differences are interpreted as simply
reflections of cultural differences among the ethnic
groups while some are attributed to differences in
levels of education and westernization.

29.   ALOBA, Abiodun.   "Journalism in Africa: 1.
Nigeria," Gazette, vol. 5, no. 2, 1959, pp. 245-248.
This article -- one of the pioneer studies on Nigerian
press published in a scholarly journal -- looks at
journalistic practice from the beginning of the press
up to the period about 1937, when the first chain
newspaper, the West African Pilot, was founded. It
particularly highlights the problems of journalism
during that early period, especially the lack of
facilities, infrastructure and personnel. But in faith

and purpose, the press was never lacking. Aspects of the law of the press are mentioned.

30. AlLOBA, Abiodun. "Journalism in Africa: II. The tabloid Revolution," Gazette, vol. 5, no. 4, 1959, pp. 409-412.
The author, a journalist who worked in the Lagos press in the 1940's, relies on personal experience to describe the press between 1948 and about 1959/1960. Special effort is made to examine the advent and effect of the Daily Mirror of London on the Nigerian press and the press in West Africa. A casual comparison is made of journalistic standards among the newspapers in former British, French and Belgian colonies in Africa. In terms of vigor, virility, freedom and circulation, the press in English-speaking Nigeria is by far superior to that in French and Belgian-speaking countries.

31. ALOBA, Abiodun. "The African Press: III. Yesterday and Today," Gazette, vol. 5, no. 3, 1959, pp. 317-321.
The third and last in a series of articles by the author, this study examines the growth of the press in West Africa with special focus on Nigeria. The role of the newspaper, radio and television in the socio-political development of Nigeria are mentioned. Special reference is also made on the introduction of the first press laws and public reaction to them.

32. ALOBA, Abiodun. "Journalism in Africa: I. Nigeria." Journalism Quarterly vol. 5, no. 1, pp. 245-248; 317-321; 409-412, 1959.
his article throws light on some of the contents of the early newspapers in Nigeria. It presents in a brief form, an overview of journalism in the country before the dawn of independence of in 1960.

33. ANASIUDU, Raphael C. The Benefits and Problems of African Countries' Participation in INTELSAT. Ph.D dissertation, University of Illinois, 1979.
An attempt to analyze the benefits and problems of African participation in INTELSAT -- the commercial satellite communication system whose facilities carry over eighty percent of the world's transcontinental public telephone communications. The main conclusion is that INTELSAT poses for African member - nations, including Nigeria, a mixture of advantages as well as disadvantages, of possibilities and challenges -- a conclusion that may not please enthusiasts who are elated by the mushrooming of INTELSAT earth stations all over Africa.

34. ANON. "A Bang on Editors' Door," Economist vol.
280, no. 7199, 1981, p. 33.
Freedom, which is the distinguishing mark of Nigerian
press, was curbed in the wake of a series of arrests
and court actions against some newspaper editors barely
three years after president Shehu Shagari's civilian
government came to power. These governmental actions
aroused fears of a more far-reaching clamp down on
centers of independent opinion in Nigeria.

35. ANON. "Press Freedom in Africa: A Huge Joke,"
Afriscope, vol. 5 (August 1975), pp. 20-21.
An analysis of freedom of the press in Africa with
special mention of press freedom in Nigeria. Although
the Nigerian press is relatively freer than the press
elsewhere in Africa, however, the author documents some
cases of arbitrary arrests, detention and physical
abuses of journalists between 1973 and 1975 to
illustrate the point that press freedom may be achieved
at a costly price.

36. ANON. "Federal Radio Corporation of Nigeria,"
Combroad, no. 40, 1979, p. 17.
A discussion of the abolition of the Nigerian
Broadcasting Corporation and the establishment of the
Federal Radio Corporation of Nigeria which ushered in a
three-tier radio broadcasting system for Nigeria: the
network news service from Lagos, broadcasting from the
zonal centers, and the service from the state stations,
termed "grass-roots broadcasting."

37. ANON. Nigerian Television Authority: Interim
Service For Calabar," Combroad, no. 43, 1979, p. 55.
A discussion of the process and problems in
establishing Nigerian Television, Calabar, which now
educates, informs, entertains and gives expression to
the rich cultural heritage of the people of Cross River
State.

38. ANON. "Federal Radio Corporation of Nigeria:
Radio and the Presidential System of Government,"
Combroad, no. 45, 1979, pp. 50-51.
The role of radio in the new political situation in
Nigeria, following the return of political power to a
democratically elected government after thirteen years
of military rule in 1979. The relationship between the
mass media and the presidential system of government is
particularly mentioned.

39. ANON. "Nigerian Television Authority: Pye
Contract," Combroad, no. 52, 1981, p. 55.

A description of the nature of one of the largest single outside broadcasting vehicles contracts received by the Pye TVT of Cambridge, England from the Nigerian Television Authority. The contract was valued at over four million British sterling pounds.

40. ANON. "Federal Radio Corporation of Nigeria: New Transmitter Complex at Ikorodu," Combroad, no. 52, 1981, pp. 54-55.
The commissioning of a Voice of Nigeria transmitter complex at Ikorodu, Lagos, in June 1981. This article also stresses the importance of an external radio service, using short-wave broadcasting, in the context of the achievement of foreign policy and international relations objectives.

41. ANON. "New Men at the top: Walter Ofonagoro - NTA (Nigeria)," Combroad, no. 58, 1983, p. 49.
A report of the appointment of Dr. Walter Ofonagoro as Director-General of Nigerian Television Authority in replacement of Vincent Maduka. A short profile of Ofonagoro is given.

42. ANON. "People: Vincent Maduka," Combroad, no. 58, 1983, p. 53.
The removal of Vincent Maduka as Director-General of Nigerian Television Authority, and his re-assignment to the Federal Ministry of Communications as special adviser by the Shehu Shagari government.

43. ANON. "Nigerian Television Authority: Uniting Nigeria Through Television," Combroad, no. 58, 1983, pp. 56-57.
Describes the stages of planning, problems and eventual transmission of television programs from Nigeria's new federal capital at Abuja by the Nigerian Television Authority. Information on staff re-assignments in the NTA is also provided.

44. ANON. "New Men at the Top: Vincent Maduka-NTA (Nigeria)," Combroad, no. 62, 1984, p. 49.
A report of a major change in the management of Nigerian Television Authority (NTA) concerning the exit of Dr. Walter Ofonagoro and the re-entry of Vincent Maduka as NTA Director-General. A brief biographic sketch of Maduka is provided.

45. ANON. "Federal Radio Corporation of Nigeria," Combroad, no. 63, 1984, pp. 52-53.
A reflection on the expanding role of the Federal Radio Corporation of Nigeria, FRCN, in the field of communication in Nigeria and other parts of Africa.

Some of the national and international activities of
the corporation's Director-General, George Bako, in the
context of radio communication are mentioned.

46. ANON. "New Men at the Top: Dahiru Modibbo (FRCN-
Nigeria)," Combroad no. 66, 1985, p. 29.
Report of a change in the Federal Radio Corporation of
Nigeria (FRCN) management, involving the appointment of
Dahiru Modibbo former Zonal Director of FRCN, Kaduna,
in the place of former boss, George Bako who retired in
December 1984. A brief profile of the new FRCN top
executive is provided.

47. ANON. "New Man at the Top." Combroad, March
1989, p. 49.
A report on the appointment of Mohammed Ibrahim as
Director- General of the Federal Radio Corporation of
Nigerian (FRCN). It is useful to journalism historians
interested in chronicling the political appointments to
top executive positions in the government-owned and
controlled Nigerian broadcasting system. The report
provides a brief profile of Mohammed Ibrahim.

48. ANON. "Northern Nigeria's Television and Sound
Broadcasting Services." E.B.U. Review, no. 80, July
1963, pp. 48-49.
A description of the progress of Northern Nigeria's
television and sound broadcasting services after two
years of operation. Three problem-areas are
highlighted.

49. ANON. "First Annual Report of the Nigerian
Broadcasting Corporation." E.B.U. Review, no. 55, June
1959, p. 18.
The first annual report of the activities of the
Nigerian Broadcasting Corporation - from january 1,
1957 to March 31, 1958.

50. ANON. "Tribalism - or Democracy?: The Role of
the Press in Africa's Way Ahead," IPI Report, vol. 9,
no. 7, 1960, pp. 7-8.
What are the prospects for freedom of the press,
freedom of speech and of assembly in the African
nations, including Nigeria that gained independence in
the 1960's? This article represents two views which
are radically opposed to one another. Mrs. Elspeth
Huxley, described by US News and World Report as 'one
of the world's foremost authorities on Africa,' is
profoundly pessimistic. Paradoxically, late Obafemi
Awolowo, one of Nigeria's top flight politicians was
optimistic. Awo believed that democracy and freedom of
speech and freedom of the press can, and should be

practiced by African nations. His views reflect
Nigerian press philosophy.

51. ANON. "Code of Ethics Planned." IPI Report, vol.
11, no. 4, 1962, p. 15.
Code of ethics approved by the Nigerian Guild of
Editors is given in this report. In pursuance of the
above, members of the Guild made an eight-point solemn
declaration, one of which reads: "we believe that it is
the duty of the journalist not to demand and to refuse
if offered any reward in cash or kind for publishing
news and comments."

52. ANON. "Nigeria's President at IPI Opening," IPI
Report, vol. 12, no. 10, 1964, pp. 3-4.
A review of the opening of the first IPI training
course in Lagos by Dr. Nnamdi Azikiwe, Nigeria's first
president who also was the founder of the country's
thriving newspaper industry of the time. Remarkable in
the review is a statement credited the ex-president:
"we in Nigeria are determined to continue to claim to
have the freest press in Africa and one of the freest
in the world."

53. ANON. "Rush For Places at NIJ," IPI Report, vol.
22, no. 2, 1973, p. 4.
A focus on the Nigerian Institute of Journalism in
Lagos. Some of its programs, facilities and intended
plans are mentioned.

54. ANON. "Nigerian Press Wants to Know...'What Did
Amakiri Do?'" IPI Report, vol. 22, nos. 9-10, 1973, pp.
1, 3, 16.
A description of the "Amakiri Affair", an incident that
marked a major watershed in the history of government-
press relations in which a Nigerian Observer reporter
was manhandled and unlawfully detained for twenty-seven
hours. Information is also provided on the reactions
of the Nigerian Observer as well as the Newspaper
Proprietor's Association of Nigerian, the Nigerian
Guild of Editors and the Nigerian Union of Journalists
to the incident.

55. ANON. "Press Freedom Report: Nigeria," IPI
Report, vol. 23, no. 1, 1974, p. 15.
An appraisal of press freedom toward the end of Yakubu
Gowon's military regime. The main conclusion is that
despite the fact that the country was under military
rule, there was a liberal government attitude toward
the press. Mention is also made of some of the facts
about the "Amakiri Affair" which serves as a major
landmark in Nigerian journalism history.

56. ANON. "The Press Under Pressure: Nigeria," IPI
Report, vol. 23, nos 4-5, 1974, p. 14.
A flash-on-the-pan account of some government-press
confrontations during the military regime of Gen.
Yakubu Gowon.

57. ANON. "Institute Affairs: Nigeria," IPI Report,
vol. 23, nos. 6-7, 1974, p. 10.
A report of the ruling on the celebrated "Amakiri
Affair" by the Magistrate Court in Port Harcourt,
presided over by Chief justice Ambrose Alagoa. The
Court awarded more than $16,000 to Minere Amakiri, the
Nigerian journalist who had his hair and beard shaved
and was ordered to be flogged by a military government
official before being detained for twenty-seven hours.
This report also provides some background on the
"Amakiri Affair" which marked a major watershed in
Nigerian journalism history.

58. ANON. "Nigeria," IPI Report, vol. 23, nos. 6-7,
1974, p. 10.
A report of victory for the rule of law in Nigeria,
following a Port Harcourt court decision to award a
total of N10,750 (About $16,000) to a Nigerian Observer
reporter, Minere Amakiri, in a suit filed against a
high-ranking military government official.

59. ANON. "The Press Under Pressure: Nigeria," IPI
Report, vol. 23, nos. 6-7, 1974, p. 12.
A brief account of press-government confrontations
during Gen. Gowon's military administration.

60. ANON. "Press Freedom in Principle, on Paper--But
in Reality ...." IPI Report, vol. 23, no. 10, 1974, p.
4.
An extract of Alhaji Lateef Jakande's speech on the
role of the mass media in a developing country. The
main thesis is that the press should be judged as a
whole, and the verdict of history must be that the mass
media in Nigeria have shown tremendous courage in the
maintenance of press freedom in the first eight years
of military rule.

61. ANON. "Press in Africa is Starved of Newsprint,"
IPI Report, vol. 23, no. 11, 1974, p. 12.
An examination of newsprint shortage in Africa's press
and its effect on journalistic practice. How Nigerian
newspapers are coping with this problem is also
examined. Particularly mentioned is the fact that this
problem is not as serious in Nigeria as in other
African countries.

62. ANON. "Spreading the Word by Satellite Has its Problems," IPI Report, vol. 23, no. 12, 1974, p. 10.
A description of satellite broadcasting systems and their special application for developing countries. Seven kinds of problems experienced in the use of television for education, particularly in Nigeria, are listed by Nigerian experts.

63. ANON. "Bitter Police and Press Exchanges in Nigeria." IPI Report, vol. 23, no. 12, 1974, p. 8.
Contains reports on some developments in relations between the Nigerian police and the press. Under renewed crusade against corruption, the Nigerian press forced a federal commissioner to resign following allegations of gross corruption. Nigerian press also accused some soldiers in power of corruption. Police issued stern warning against false reports but Nigerian press was unruffled by the warning.

64. ANON. "Nigerian Reaction to Board Move," IPI Report, vol. 24, nos. 4-5, 1975, p. 8.
This article ventilates our understanding of how the Nigerian press views the policy of apartheid government in South Africa. It particularly throws some light on the reaction of the print media, especially the Daily Sketch, New Nigerian and Daily Times, to the International Press Institute's principle that South African journalists should be free to attend an IPI General Assembly in Lagos in 1975.

65. ANON. "Lagos General Assembly Cancellation Executive Board Statement," IPI Report, vol. 24, nos. 4-5, 1975, p. 8.
What were the circumstances that led to the cancellation of an International Press Institute (IPI) General Assembly slated for Lagos, and the holding of the Assembly in Zurich, may 12 and 13, 1975? This article analyzes the political issues in the decision that led to the re-scheduling of the venue for the Assembly of the international press.

66. ANON. "Nigerian Press - Articulate and Fearless," IPI Report, vol. 24, no. 6, 1975, p. 1.
An extract of the comment by Babatunde Jose, then editor of the Daily Times on the International Press Institute's decision to switch assembly venue from Lagos to Zurich, following Nigerian government's refusal to issue entry visas to South African IPI members. The crux of Jose's comment is that despite being under military rule, the Nigerian press has continued to be virile, courageous, articulate and fearless.

An Annotated Bibliography

67. ANON. "Degrees: A Passport to Journalism?" IPI
Report, vol. 24, no. 8, 1975, pp. 9-10.
This article addresses the issue of journalism
education and journalistic competence in African media
with special focus on Nigeria. The views of two well
respected journalism educators in Nigeria -- professors
Fred Omu and Ezenta Eze both heads of department of
mass Communications at two Nigerian universities --are
highlighted.

68. ANON. "Oath-Taking Newsmen Back Ethics Code," IPI
Report, vol. 28, no. 6, 1979, pp. 7, 10.
How would journalists fare after the return to civilian
government in 1979? How could their status be enhanced
within the context of the changing political directions
in the country? These are the major questions
considered in this article. An eight-point code of
conduct adopted by the Nigerian Press Organization is
fully described.

69. ANON. "Nigerian Editors Call For an End to Mass
Staff Purges," IPI Report, vol. 29, no. 3, 1980, p. 4.
This piece contains an account of the proceedings of
the Nigerian Guild of Editor's (NGE) annual conference
in Calabar during which Nigerian journalists demanded
better access to government information and a halt in
the military government's interest in two national
dailies -- the Daily Times and New Nigerian.

70. ANON. "World Press Freedom Review: Nigeria," IPI
Report, vol. 29, no. 6, 1980, p. 12.
An appraisal of press freedom in the first year of
Alhaji Shehu Shagari's civilian administration. The
picture presented is that the Shagari government was
ready to open the door for freedom of expression at
least, as exemplified in the administration's
instruction to immigration officials not to ban any
foreign correspondents entering the country.

71. ANON. "African Pilot - End of an Era." IPI
Report, Vol. 30, no. 6, 1981, p. 15.
Reports on the death of one of the oldest privately
owned newspapers in West Africa, the West African
Pilot, published in Lagos, by the doyen of West African
politics and journalism, Dr. Nnamdi Azikiwe. The death
of the Pilot is, however, lamented on account of its
significant role in the nationalist struggle of the
1940-50; 1950-60 periods and for providing on-the-job
training for the country's newsmen.

72. ANON. "Newspaper Arrest - Shagari Hits Back." IPI
Report, vol. 30, no. 7, 1981, p. 2.

17

Nigerian president, Alhaji Shehu Shagari, denies
reprots of police arrests of newspaper editors and
executives but notes that the government had not told
the police to arrest anyone. Police action against six
newspaper editors and one managing director followed
published reports of allegation that Shagari had tried
to bribe some opposition politicians.

73. ANON. "World Press Freedom Review: Nigeria," IPI
Report, vol. 31, nos. 1 & 2, 1981/2, pp. 16-17.
An end-of-year review of the state of press freedom in
Nigeria. This article catalogues incidents of arrests,
detentions, trials and general harassment of
journalists in 1981.

74. ANON. "World Press Freedom Review," IPI Report,
vol. 32, no. 12, 1983, pp. 7-24.
An appraisal of the state of press freedom in eighty-
nine countries, including Nigeria which is also listed
in the country index. A gloomy picture is painted for
the Nigerian press in the wake of the 1983 elections.
The tribulations of the media -- print and electronic
-- are highlighted.

75. ANON. "Nigeria: Curb Threat by President," IPI
Report, vol. 33, no. 3, 1984, p. 13.
Maj. Gen. Muhammadu Buhari, head of the Federal
Military Government threatens that press freedom
provisions in the suspended Constitution would be
revised because "Nigeria's press was capable of abusing
its freedom to the extent of endangering stability."

76. ANON. "Blowing the Whistle on Mercenary
Journalists," IPI Report, vol. 33, no. 4, 1984, p. 13.
Even though the Nigerian Press may be regarded as the
freest in Africa, it is by no means as free or as
responsible as it should or could be. This is because
the "Mearly Mouthedness" of the Charlatans in the press
who, out of overzealous instincts, turn the ethical
principles upside down and throw objectivity out of the
columns of the press.

77. ANON. "Nigeria: Fears For the Future as Two Are
Jailed," IPI Report, vol. 33, no. 8, 1984, pp. 1, 10.
A report of the arrest, detention and imprisonment of
two editors of the Guardian under the provisions of
Decree no. 4 enacted by the Buhari military government
in 1984. A detailed account of the legal fireworks and
counter arguments at the trial of the journalists is
provided along with reactions from the International
Press Institute regarding the imprisonment of
journalists by the Buhari government.

An Annotated Bibliography

78. ANON. "World Press Freedom Review: Nigeria," IPI
Report, vol. 33, no. 12, 1984, p. 14.
An appraisal of the state of freedom of the press in
Nigeria by the close of 1984. Names of journalists
detained as well as newspapers punished are provided.
The main conclusion is that the entry of the Buhari
military regime to political power in December 1983,
severely restricted what was once the freest press in
Africa.

79. ANON. "Nigerian Cut-Back," IPI Report, vol. 34,
no. 4, 1985, p. 24.
A reflection on the impact of Nigeria's economic hard
times on the press and journalistic practice.
Information is provided on the number of media workers
retrenched as a result of continued national economic
turbulence.

80. ANON. "No Licence, No Print...," IPI Report, vol.
34, no. 8, 1985, p. 11.
An account of the impact of newsprint crisis on
Nigerian newspaper industry, and the government's plan
to end the crisis.

81. ANON. "End of the Line," IPI Report, vol. 34, no.
8, 1985, p. 11.
A report of the death of The Democrat, one of Nigeria's
two broadsheet weekly (Sunday) newspapers. The
Democrat, established on December 31, 1983, was
officially shut down on April 19, 1985, and the last
edition was published on April 21.

82. ANON. "New Regime Releases Former IPI Chairman,"
IPI Report, volume 34, no. 10, 1985, p. 1.
A report of the release of Nigerian journalists,
including the former chairman of the International
Press Institute, Lateef jakande, from jail after twenty
months. Reference is also made of Decree no. 4 of 1984
and Nigerian press freedom.

83. ANON. "World Press Freedom Review: Nigeria," IPI
Report, vol. 34, no. 12, 1985, p.
A review of some of the measures, including economic
actions, utilized by the Buhari military government to
tame the Nigerian press. The impact of the measures on
journalistic performance is also reviewed. The main
conclusion is that the abrogation of those measures by
the Babangida military regime clearly provided a
climate for vigorous expression to flourish, a virtue
normally associated with the Nigerian press.

84. ANON. "Contempt Questioned," IPI Report, vol. 35, no. 7, 1986, pp. 6-7.
The conviction of Ray Ekpu, deputy editor-in chief of the Newswatch magazine by a Lagos Tribunal headed by Justice Uwaifo, provides the opportunity for the author to take a look at the law of contempt which is becoming irrelevant in legal circles.

85. ANON. "Mystery as Parcel bomb Kills Nigerian Editor," IPI Report, vol. 35, no. 11, 1986, p. 5.
A description of the circumstances surrounding the death of Dele Giwa, editor of the privately owned Newswatch weekly magazine. This article also profiles Dele Giwa, and provides some account of public and government reactions to the incident.

86. ANON. "World Press Freedom Review: Nigeria," IPI Report, vol. 35, no. 12, 1986, p. 22.
This article assesses the state of freedom of the press by the end of 1986. A picture of cordial government-press relations is painted. President Ibrahim Babangida's abrogation of the hated Decree No. 4 of 1984, and his improvement of human rights and civil liberties, appeared to have sparked new life into the press. The article also provides information on the circumstances surrounding the death of Dele Giwa, editor of the weekly Newswatch.

87. ANON. "Newswatch Ban Is Lifted Early," IPI Report, vol. 36, no. 9, 1987, p. 2.
A report of the Federal Military Government's lifting of the six-month ban which it imposed on the weekly news magazine, Newswatch, for publishing a leaked report commissioned by President Ibrahim Babangida to examine the possibility of a return to civilian rule in 1990.

88. ANON. "Security Officers to be Prosecuted in Dele Giwa Murder Case," IPI Report, vol. 37, no. 2, 1988, p. 9.
A description of the facets of the legal battle in the Dele Giwa case in which the Supreme Court made legal history, approving a move to institute a private prosecution against two of the country's top security officers for the parcel bomb murder of Dele Giwa, Newswatch, editor.

89. ANON. "Giwa Fight Will Go On," IPI Report, vol. 37, no. 4, 1988, pp. 9-10.
A summary of a Lagos High Court's ruling on a law suit brought against two officers of the Nigerian Army by Chief Gani Fawehinmi in connection with the parcel bomb

murder of Dele Giwa, <u>Newswatch</u> editor. Defence
counsel's submissions and the court's reasoning on the
suit are also summarized.

90. ANON. "Government Bans Satellite Dishes," <u>IPI
Report</u>, vol. 37, no. 4, 1988, p. 10.
A report of the Federal Military Government's ban of
the use of satellite antennas for receiving foreign
broadcasts. This report also highlights the rationale
for the government's action.

91. ANON. "Nigeria," <u>Index on Censorship</u>, vol. 13,
no. 3, 1984, p. 47.
A Report of the Federal Military Government Publication
of a decree which empowered it to make laws, including
press laws that could not be challenged in the court,
thus modifying the Constitution which was partially
suspended when the civilian government of Shehu Shagari
was toppled in a coup d'etat on December 31, 1983.
This piece also contains information on the detention
of Malam Haroun Adamu, editorial consultant of the
privately owned <u>Punch</u> by officials of the military
government.

92. ANON. "Nigeria," <u>Index on Censorship</u>, vol. 13,
no. 4, 1984, p. 42.
Provides information on the publication of a new press
law --Decree No. 4, of 1984 which gave the military
government of Maj. Gen. Buhari powers to close
newspapers and radio/television stations as well as
jail journalists for reporting false statements. A
summary of the decree's provisions is given. A short
chronological account of journalists detained or
punished under the provisions of the decree is also
provided.

93. ANON. "Nigeria: Dr. Tai Solarin," <u>Index on
Censorship</u>, vol. 13, no. 5, 1984, pp. 41-42.
The arrest and imprisonment of Dr. Tai Solarin, a
veteran educationist, social critic and newspaper
columnist by the military authorities. The arrest was
in connection with newspaper articles written by Dr.
Solarin in the <u>Sunday Tribune</u> and <u>Nigerian Tribune</u> of
February 26 and March 12, 1984 respectively in which he
criticized the Buhari military government's policy on
the detention of politicians.

94. ANON. "Nigeria," <u>Index on Censorship</u>, vol. 13.
no. 6, 1984, p. 46.
A report on the release of Idowu Odeyemi, a journalist
arrested and detained by the Mohammadu Buhari military
government.

95. ANON. "Nigeria," Index on Censorship, Vol. 14, no. 1, 1985, p. 63.
A report of the invasion of the privately-owned Punch on September 14, 1984 by military officials said to be irate over stories carried in the newspaper on September 11 and 13. Information on the release of two hundred and fifty detainees, including Chigozie Ozim, editor of the Enugu-based Sunday Satellite newspaper, is also contained in this report.
   Also provided is information on the arrest and detention on November 9, 1984, of Duro Onabule, editor of the privately-owned National Concord for his newspaper commentary titled "Bogey of Bringing Down Government."

96. ANON. "Nigeria," Index on Censorship, vol. 14, no. 2, 1985, p. 55.
A report of the arrest and detention of Rufai Ibrahim, former acting editor of The Guardian at his residence by officers of the Nigerian Security Organization (NSO). A court ruling on an appeal filed by the Nigerian Union of Journalists (NUJ), challenging the constitutionality of Decree No. 4 of 1984 is also reported.

97. ANON. "Nigeria," Index On Censorship, vol. 14, no. 3, 1985, p. 51.
Contains a report of the release of two senior editors of the Guardian, Tunde Thompson and Nduka Irabor, who were jailed on July 4, 1984 by a military court for contravening Decree No. 4 of 1984.

98. ANON. "Nigeria," Index on Censorship, Vol. 14, no. 5, 1985, p. 67.
A report about a long-standing government order prohibiting interviews by civil service workers with foreign media. The order had been extended to academics.

99. ANON. "Nigeria," Index on Censorship, vol. 14, no. 1, 1986, pp. 21-24.
A description of the writing of Sam Ikoku -- one of Nigeria's irrepressible writers and politician who once stood for election against his father, Sir Alvan Ikoku. In his book, Ikoku advanced complex ideas on how Nigeria could be saved from dictatorship. The book was banned, and Ikoku was arrested and thrown into jail by the military government.

100. ANON. "Nigeria," Index on Censorship, vol. 15, no. 3, 1986, p. 39.

An Annotated Bibliography

An account of a <u>Daily Times</u> editorial welcoming an
announcement by the Ibrahim Babangida military
government that senior civil service workers could talk
to the press on issues within their competence -- after
they had been prohibited (by the military regime) from
making "unauthorized" statements to the press. Some
implications of the new policy vis-a-vis debates on
issues of public interest are mentioned.

101. ANON. "Nigeria," <u>Index on Censorship</u>, vol. 15,
no. 6, 1986, p. 39.
This piece contains a report on three leaders of the
United Christian Association who were facing charges of
causing 'a breach of public peace' after they had
distributed posters relating to the Organization of the
Islamic Conference. This piece also contains
information on the release of Afrobeat musician and
social commentator, Fela Anikulapo Kuti, after spending
twenty months in jail. He was sentenced in September
1984 to five years imprisonment for what many felt was
due to his acerbic criticism of successive Nigerian
governments.

102. ANON. "Nigeria," <u>Index on Censorship</u>, vol. 15,
no. 7, 1986, p. 43.
A report of a criticism of British Broadcasting
Corporation (BBC) stereotyped coverage of student
unrest in Nigeria earlier in the year (May). The
criticism is made by the chief press secretary of
president Ibrahim Babangida, Duro Onabule.

103. ANON. "Nigeria," <u>Index on Censorship</u>, vol. 15,
no. 8, 1986, p. 39.
This is a report on the amendment of Decree no. 2 of
1984 (State Security and Detention of Persons),
providing for up to six months renewable detention of
anyone, including journalists without charge or trial.
Also contained in this report is information on the
continued detention of Dr. Junaid Mohammed, former
member of the proscribed People's Redemption Party who
was arrested on May 27, 1986 following the broadcast of
his interview on BBC (London) in which he criticized
maj. Gen. Babangida's military government.

104. ANON. "Nigeria," <u>Index on Censorship</u>, vol. 15,
no. 10, 1986, p. 47.
An account of the release of Dr. Junaid Mohammed who
was arrested on May 27, 1986 following an interview he
gave to a British Broadcasting Corporation (BBC)
correspondent in Kano in which he criticized the
military government of Maj. Gen. Ibrahim Babangida.

105. ANON. "Nigeria," Index on Censorship, vol. 16,
no. 8 (Sept. 1987), p. 38.
A report of the detention and deportation of Ray
Wilkinson, a Newsweek correspondent in Lagos.

106. ANON. "Nigeria," Index on Censorship, vol. 16,
no. 6, (June) 1987, p. 38.
A report of the closure of the news magazine,
Newswatch, by military authorities on April 6, 1987,
for publishing confidential report on the country's
political future.

107. ANON. "Nigerian Magazine Closed," Index on
Censorship, vol. 16, no. 6 (June) 1987, pp. 4-5.
An analysis of the circumstances that led to the
closure of Newswatch magazine on April 6, 1987,
following a military order issued by Rear-Admiral
Augustus Aikhomo, Chief of General Staff of the Armed
Forces. The reactions of the public, especially the
Nigerian Bar Association, Association of Nigerian
Authors, the Nigerian Union of Journalists and
university campuses, are also mentioned.

108. ANON. "Nigeria: One Year of Military Rule,"
West Africa, no. 3514 (December 24/31, 1984), pp. 2616-
2618.
An evaluation of Maj. Gen. Buhari's first year in
office. Reference is made to Decree No. 4 of 1984 with
respect to the military government's relationship with
the press. The major point made in the article is that
the decree strained government-press relations, and may
have had the advantage of sharpening the debate on the
role of the press in Nigeria.

109. ANON. "The Immigrant Expulsion," West Africa,
no. 3534 (May 20, 1985), p. 990.
How did the press in Ghana and Nigeria react to the
expulsion of immigrants from Nigeria? Comments from
the New Nigerian, National Concord, The Guardian, Daily
Times, Ghana Radio, and The Free Press of Ghana tend to
condemn the Nigerian government action.
For the opinions of the press on some other domestic
and foreign issues, see e.g. West Africa, no. 3525
(March 18, 1985) pp. 510-511; West Africa, no. 3530
(April 22, 1985), p. 779.

110. ANON. "Thirty Years of NUJ," West Africa, no.
3536 (June 3, 1985), pp. 1101-1103.
The celebration of the 30th anniversary of the Nigerian
Union of Journalists was an occasion to reflect on some
of the domestic and foreign issues that the press has
been involved in.

111. ANON. "The State of Emergency," <u>West Africa</u>, no.
3545 (August 5, 1985), p. 1586.
A report of the editorial positions of Nigerian and
Western newspapers on the state of emergency imposed in
1985 by the apartheid regime in South Africa. The
newspapers covered in this report include: <u>The Mirror</u>,
<u>The Guardian</u> and <u>Financial Times</u> of London, <u>Le Monde</u> of
Paris, <u>The Washington Post</u> and <u>New York Times</u> of U.S.A.
The <u>Daily Times</u> and <u>The Guardian</u> of Lagos are the
Nigerian newspapers covered in the report.

112. ANON. "Nigeria: Babangida Takes Over," <u>West
Africa</u>, no. 3549 (September 2, 1985).
Reference is made to the institutional control measure
-- Decree no. 4 of 1984 -- adopted by the Buhari regime
to tame the press. This report also contains Maj. Gen.
Ibrahim Babangida's maiden address in which Decree no.
4 of 1984 was repealed, and all journalists released
from detention.

113. ANON. <u>A List of American Doctoral Dissertations
on Africa</u>. Washington, D. C.: Library of Congress,
n.d.
A sixty-nine-page reference book on doctoral
dissertations written on Africa in American
universities. Only one dissertation directly touching
on the Nigerian press (by Michael Traber) is listed.
However, some of the works listed on constitutional
development and nationalism such as that by James S.
Coleman, make references to the press.

114. ANON. "UNESCO Plans to Develop Mass Media in
Africa," <u>Journalism Quarterly</u>, vol. 39, no. 2, 1962, p.
215.
A Report on major decisions reached at a two-week
UNESCO conference in its Paris headquarters, toward
mass media development in African countries, including
Nigeria. More than a hundred representatives from
thirty-two countries, including Nigeria attended the
media development conference.

115. ANON. "A Newsroom Unlike Any Other: IFJ Seminar
Sharpens Skills of West African Journalists," <u>The
Journalist's World</u>, no. 1, 1964, pp. 2-7.
A report of a three-week long journalism course
organized by the International Federation of
Journalists for twenty-eight West African journalists
from Sierra Leone and Nigeria held in 1964 at the
University Ibadan, Nigeria.

116. ANON. "Pulp and Paper Industries in Nigeria: A
Situational Analysis." Nigerian Trade Journal, vol.
22, no. 4, 1975, pp. 12-16.
This article attempts to analyze the development and
consumption of pulp and paper in Nigeria. Newsprint
consumption is low. Production is also minimal.
Importation is high. Problems and plans for newsprint
production in the country are discussed.

117. ANON. "What the Papers Say." West Africa, no.
3305, 1980, pp. 2357-2359.
A correspondent in Lagos reports on how the Nigerian
press handled the twentieth independence anniversary
and the first anniversary of civilian rule. Nigerian
press editorials on the anniversary reflected party
loyalties of newspapers, but also gave some
professionally objective assessments of the country's
past failures and future problems.

118. ANON. "Assessing Nigeria's Newspapers." West
Africa, no. 3287, 1980, pp. 1337-1339.
A comment on the quality of Nigerian journalists and
media by chief Michael Asaju, president of the Nigerian
Union of Journalists in a speech to the graduates of
the short term reporting class of the Nigerian
Institute of Journalism in Lagos. Many newspapers in
Nigeria are state-owned, and have become state
government megaphones. Most of the newspapers and
their journalists are rebuked for failing standards of
professionalism. Television is the only sector of the
media where high journalistic standards are practiced.
Some problems of Nigerian journalism are also
highlighted.

119. ANON. "Why Writers Need an Association." West
Africa, no. 3339, 1981, pp. 1692-1694.
An opening address by Chinua Achebe, the Nigerian
novelist, at the convention of Nigerian authors held at
the University of Nigeria, Nsukka, June 1981. Achebe
regrets that the Society of Nigerian Authors (SONA) was
defunct and calls for the formation of an association
of Nigerian writers.

120. ANON. Commercial Radio in Africa. Federal
Republic of Germany: German African Society, 1970.
A handbook of broadcasting and television broadcasting
stations in Africa, basically intended for advertisers
and marketers in African countries, including Nigeria.
Data for each station listed includes official names,
addresses of stations, language or languages in which
commercials are broadcast, advertising rates, special

regulations, services, coverage, transmitting power and wave length.

121. ANYADIKE, Nnamdi. "What Price Press Freedom?" Index on Censorship, vol. 14, no. 2, 1985, pp. 39-42. Author looks at the state of press freedom under the Mohammadu Buhari military regime which began on December 31, 1983. Brief accounts of press laws enacted by the regime, the enforcement of the laws and their implications in the context of freedom of the press and growth of Nigerian media are given. The main conclusion is that with the enforcement of the press laws enacted by Buhari, the future of freedom of the press would largely depend on how much more ruthless and efficient dictatorship the military regime was prepared to be.

122. ANYAKA, Chuma J. The Cultural Form of Television in Anambra State, Nigeria. Ph.D dissertation, New York University, 1986. This study analyzes the cultural form of the Nigerian Television Authority, Channel 8 (NTA-8), a network station in Anambra state. It also examines the history and structure of prime time programming, the metamessages communicated by the structure of programming, and the perceptions and uses of the television by its adult audience.

123. ANYANDELE, E. A. "The Phenomenon of Visionary Nationalists in Precolonial Nigeria," In J.E. Flint, & G. Williams (Eds.), Perspectives of Empires (pp. 112-129). London: Longman Group Ltd., 1973. Describes public expression and press comments on some British colonial policies in Lagos Colony. When the colonial government sought to introduce taxation without representation, for example, the educated African elites and press expressed the view that taxation be introduced with representation. According to the author, Thomas Paine's principles of "The Rights of Man," and the American Revolution gave special meaning to the educated African elites and the press in their opposition against colonial policy on taxation.

124. ARIDEGBE, Olufemi. "Broadcasting Autonomy in Nigeria, 1932-82: An Interpretative History." M.S. thesis, University of Tennessee, Knoxville, 1984. An attempt to provide a historical analysis of broadcasting autonomy in Nigeria from 1932 to 1982. Author contends that the Nigerian Broadcasting corporation in the post-colonial era failed to integrate broadcasting to serve the common purpose of the populace because of certain social and political

factors. Recommendations are made on how the broadcasting industry and future governments can relate under the ideals of democracy.

125. ARMS, George. "Diary From Nigeria: Strides Made in One Year," NAEB Journal, September-October 1961, pp. 11-21.
This article is a part of the author's series on the development of educational broadcasting in Nigeria. Specifically, it describes the beginning of the first television station in Africa -- Western Nigeria Television (WNTV-WNBS) -- started in Ibadan in 1959.

126. ARMS, George L. "Diary From Nigeria: The Second Year." NAEB Journal, January/February 19863, pp. 9-14.
A follow up of author's earlier article in 1961. This article focuses on efforts to train Nigerian television staff.

127. ARMS, George. "Diary From Nigeria: The Third Year," NAEB Journal, March-April 1964, pp. 25-32.
This article which focuses on a USAID-supported educational television project, is the last in a series of reports on various aspects of educational broadcasting in Nigeria.

128. ARMSTRONG, Robert P. "The University Press in a Developing Country." Scholarly Publishing, vol. 5, no. 1, 1973, pp. 35-40.
A discussion on the role of a university press as an important cultural medium in a developing country, using Nigeria as an example. Scholarly presses play a vital role in shaping and encouraging intellectual efforts.

129. ASCROFT, Joseph R. et. al. Patterns of Diffusion in Rural Eastern Nigeria. Diffusion of Innovation Research Report, no. 11. East Lansing: Michigan State University, Department of Communication, 1969.
This study conducted by Michigan State University mass communication scholars examines the patterns of introducing and diffusing information on new ideas (innovation) in Eastern Nigeria.

130. ASEIN, Samuel O. "Literature and Society in Lagos." Nigeria Magazine, nos. 117-118, 1975, pp. 22-32.
This article traces missionary activity in Nigeria and missionaries' attempt to educate Africans about European culture, in part by means of essay competitions, which led to the development of a new

An Annotated Bibliography

class of African writers, "black victorians" and other journalists in the country.

131. ASPINAL, Richard. Radio Programme Production: A Manual For Training. Paris: UNESCO, 1971.
Provides information on the type of broadcast training curricula commonly taken by most African countries, including Nigeria.

132. ATTAH, Ben E. "An Analysis of Polymorphic Opinion Leadership In Eastern Nigerian Communities," M.A. thesis, Michigan State University, 1968.
The author seeks to examine the various types of opinion leaders, and concludes that polymorphic opinion leadership is not a characteristic limited only in the former eastern region of Nigeria.

133. AXINN, George H., & nancy W. Axinn. "Rural Communications: Preliminary Findings of a Nigerian Study," Rural Africana, no. 8, 1968, pp. 19-21.
The authors describe the findings of a study of communication patterns of rural inhabitants in Nigeria. A later report of this study is published in the authors' work in Journalism Quarterly. In this very study, the authors note that most communication among rural dwellers is on interpersonal level. Men read more, while women tend to talk more.

134. AXINN, George H., & Nancy W. Axinn, "Communication Among the Nsukka Ibgo: A folk-Village Society," Journalism Quarterly, vol. 46, no. 2, 1969, pp. 320-324, 406.
A description of the communication behavior of the rural people living around Nsukka -- site of Nigeria's premier journalism college. Data for the year-long study which were collected by diary and interview methods, show that residents of the area devote a smaller proportion of their time to radio listening an/or reading than do others in more developed communities. They devote more time to listening to one another than attending to mass mediated communication.

135. AYENI, Dipo. "An Expanded Educational Radio Broadcasting System in Nigeria," Combroad, no. 62, 1984, pp. 20-23.
An examination of educational radio program, program ideas and scheduling of such programs to the benefit of Nigerian listeners. The present level of operation as well as some problems of educational broadcasting such as ethnic diversity, language, culture, religion and norms, are also examined. A strong case is made for the use of expanded educational radio broadcasting

29

system, involving state and federal ministries,
community development agencies, cooperative societies
and trade unions in national development, particularly
in creating and in inculcating a sense of new social
order and new social values, including ethical
orientation within society.

136. AYO-VAUGHAN, Sam F. "Africa's First TV," The
Journalists World, vol. 5, nos. 3-4, 1967, pp. 4-5.
A brief account of the first television station in
tropical Africa -- the Western Nigerian Television
(WNTV) in Ibadan.

137. AZIKIWE, Nnamdi. "Journalism in West Africa,"
West African Pilot, May 18-June 13, 1945.
Dr. Nnamdi Azikiwe, one of Nigeria's pioneer
journalists, presents twenty-two articles which
appeared in the series cited in the Pilot above.
Although these article appeared in a newspaper, they
are being specially listed in this work not only
because they are as good as some works listed in some
journals but also for what a pioneer Nigerian
journalist who later became first ceremonial president
of Nigeria has to say in one of his chain of newspapers
about the role of the Nigerian press in agitational
politics during the colonial era.

138. AZIKIWE, Nnamdi, ZIK: Selected Speeches of Dr.
Nnamdi Azikiwe. London: Cambridge University Press,
1961.
A selection from the speeches of Governor-General of
the Federation of Nigeria and first ceremonial
president, Dr. Nnamdi Azikiwe, founder of the West
African Pilot, the newspaper at the forefront of the
movement for nationalism in Nigeria. Among the items
listed are his speech in the House of Representatives
on August 23, 1954 on the Nigerian Broadcasting
Corporation, and his address in the Eastern Nigerian
house of Assembly on March 29, 1955, in which he moved
the Second Reading of a Bill for "A Law to regulate the
publication and distribution of newspapers in the
former eastern region to register newspapers and news
agents."

139. AZIKIWE, Nnamdi. "Pioneer Heroes of the Nigerian
Press." Lecture delivered in honor of the first
graduating students of the Jackson College of
Journalism, University of Nigeria, Nsukka, May 31,
1964.
The author, first ceremonial President of Nigeria and
one of greatest Nigerian journalists, draws attention
to the works of pioneer heroes of the Nigerian Press.

A brief history of the newspaper press, especially the
Iwe Irohin is presented.

140. BAKO, George. "Reorganization and Future
Development of Radio Broadcasting in Nigeria,"
Combroad, no. 42, 1977, pp. 7-9.
The future of broadcasting in Nigeria will continue to
be directly related to the political and cultural
development of the country. Radio broadcasting will
continue to change as long as the nation moves
positively in order to reflect the aspirations, needs
and requirements of the people of Nigeria.

141. BAKO, George. "Future of Broadcasting in
Nigeria," Combroad, no. 58, 1983, pp. 5-8.
Author's main thesis is that the future of broadcasting
in Nigeria hinges on the effective management of
frequency allocation and the subsequent regulation in
broad terms of the content of programs. Subjects such
as private broadcast stations, frequency allocation and
commercial broadcast stations, frequency allocation and
commercial broadcasting are also discussed. The future
of broadcasting, author contends, is bright.

142. BALEWA, Saddik. "Nigeria's Film Industry," West
Africa, no. 3513 (December 17, 1984), pp. 2583-4.
Former chief executive of the Nigerian film
corporation, Adamu Halilu, reflects on the state of the
film industry and prospects for the future.
Also in this same issue of West Africa, a Nigerian
movie critic looks at a program shown on British
television which highlighted the discrimination faced
by African-American actors in the U.S. film industry.

143. BAMIDURO, Stephen O. The Politics of the Nigerian
Press: An Analysis of Press Viewpoints on Three
Fundamental Issues of Post-Independence Politics, 1960-
1965 Ph.D dissertation, The John Hopkins University,
1981.
This study investigates the impact of the social milieu
on press behavior through the analysis of the
viewpoints of the Nigerian press on three fundamental
issues of post-independence politics between 1960 and
1965. The development of the Nigerian press between
1859 and 1945 is also discussed. Key issues in this
period are briefly analyzed to determine the pattern of
interaction between the press and its social milieu.

144. BARRETT, Lindsay. "Return of the Military 5: New
People New Issues," West Africa, no. 3494 (August 6,
1984), pp.1573-4.

The conclusion of a series of articles on Nigeria, with
an assessment of the performance of the Buhari regime.
Reference is made to Decree no. 4 of 1984 with respect
to Buhari's sense of fair play. The real test of the
government's sense of fair play will be seen in the
extent to which it might use this decree to silence
legitimate and well reasoned critical opinion.

145. BARTON, Frank. The Press of Africa: Persecution
and Perseverance. New York: Africana Publishing
Company, 1979.
An overview of the history and development of the press
in Africa. Statistical data on mass media in Nigeria
is provided along with information on some of the major
newspapers, Nigerian Guild of Editors, Nigerian Union
of Journalists, history and freedom of the press.

146. BASS, Abraham Z. "Promoting Nationhood Through
Television in Africa." Journal of Broadcasting, Vol.
13, no, 2, 1969, pp. 163-166.
This article contains the opinions of directors-general
and other top television executives from nine African
countries regarding the roles of television in their
countries. The Nigerian official interviewed for the
study explained the role of NIgerian broadcasting: "To
reflect the strength and diversity of all those things
that go to make Nigeria what it is; it is expected to
raise the standard of understanding, satisfy differing
cultures and foster the growth of ethical values and
the feeling of nationhood."

147. Benn's Press Directory: Volume 2. London: Benn
Publications limited, 1978.
Begun in 1877, this publication -- now in its 126th
edition -- provides valuable information on the press
outside United Kingdom. Included in this volume are
information resources and publicity channels in
Nigeria. Names and addresses of radio, television and
newspaper houses are given. Information on radio and
television is not thorough but it provides one of the
most complete listings of Nigerian periodicals and
their addresses.

148. BLED. Cynthia E. "Review of Audience Research in
Some Developing Countries of Africa." Journal of
Broadcasting, Vol. 23, no. 2, 1969, pp. 167-180.
This article which synthesizes information received
through correspondence, discussion and literature
searching, is based upon a larger document prepared by
the author for the Canadian Broadcasting Corporation.
It provides some information on the limitations of
communicating in American English to Nigerian students

unaccustomed to the accents. It also contains the
recommendations of a UNESCO-sponsored conference on the
introduction and development of television in Africa,
held in Lagos, September 1964.

149. BOAFO, Kwame S.T. "Utilizing Development
Communication Strategies in African Societies: A
Critical Perspective (Development Communication in
Africa)," Gazette, vol. 35, no. 2, 1985, pp. 83-92.
Although this study is generally focused on sub-Saharan
Africa, it provides information on mass communication
and rural development in Nigeria. For example, it
contends that radio has been utilized to tackle
development problems in health, education, agriculture
and other sectors of development in Nigeria. In
addition to radio, experiments using rural newspapers,
television and traditional media, in combination with
small group discussions, for literacy development,
family planning education and social change, have been
undertaken in Nigeria.

150. BOAHEN, Adu A. (ed.), General History of Africa,
VII: Africa Under Colonial Domination 1880-1935.
Berkely, California: University of California Press,
1985.
The general focus of this book is on Africa under
colonial domination from 1880 to 1935. Information is
provided on the role of the African press, including
Nigerian newspapers in African politics and nationalism
between 1919 and 1935. Specific mention is made of
some Lagos newspapers.

151. BOWER, Roger. "In Nigeria Talent is Easiest
Problem," Broadcasting. May 25, 1964, pp. 106-107.
Author, a member of the National Broadcasting Company
contract team, briefly describes the origins of
Nigerian federal television service.

152. BOWMAN, Marvin. "The First Year of Educational
Television In Lagos, Nigeria," CETO News, no. 13,
December, 1966, pp. 22-26.
A description of the first year of instructional
television in the Federal Television station, Lagos.

153. BROOKE, James. "Who Killed Giwa?" IPI Report,
vol. 36, no. 1, 1987, p. 13.
An attempt to examine the circumstance that surrounded
the parcel-bomb murder of Dele Giwa. A flash-on-the-
pan profile of Giwa is also made.

154.   BROWNE, Don R. "Radio in Africa: Problems and
Prospects." NAEB Review, vol. 22, no. 6, 1963, pp. 32-
35.
A discussion of problems and prospects of radio
broadcasting in Africa that is useful for a study of
broadcasting in Nigeria.

155.   BRUCE, Augustus M. "Social Political Developments
Seen in African Press." IPI Report, vol. 6, no. 8,
1957, p. 8.
The author reviews one of the books on various phases
of African press, The Press in Africa, written by Helen
Kitchen. Unlike most African countries, indigenous
newspapers in Nigeria such as the West African Pilot,
the Daily Service and a host of other papers attracted
well-educated African staff all along.

156.   BURKHART, Ford. "Nigeria: Tribalism Fosters
Free-Press Value in US-Style System." Quill, vol. 71,
no. 3, 1983, pp. 6-12.
This article mirrors the state of Nigerian press since
the military handed over power to civilians in 1979.
The press is vigorous and free. First Amendment
principles and American-style press freedom are written
into the Nigerian Constitution. Tribalism may have
contributed as much as any other factor to the climate
of press freedom in Nigeria. The multiplicity of press
outlets has kept the five political parties from
bottling up the media. Although the press has
performed well so far, there have been one or two
instances of blunders, such as the `oilgate' scandal: a
news report that five billion dollars in oil revenue
was embezzled by some government officials.

157.   BURNS, Alan. History of Nigeria. London: George
Allen and Unwin Ltd., 1963.
History of modern Nigeria. Contains information on the
first newspaper, Iwe Irohin, as well as the activities
of the press in the movement for nationalism. For
example, the author points out instances during which
the press encouraged and directed labor and political
unrest as well as whipping up anti-European sentiments
and exacerbating racial prejudice.

158.   CHICK, John D. "The Nigerian Press and National
Integration," Journal of Commonwealth Political
Studies, vol. 9, no. 2, 1971, pp. 115-133.
An inquiry into the influence of the Nigerian press on
internal divisiveness. The press tends to be virulent
in expression, but regional and sociopolitical
limitations modify its national influence and
effectiveness. it is not possible to precisely

determine the extent of press influence on individual
conceptualization but newspapers are customarily
considered by both their supporters and opponents as
exercising a greater impact than is indeed the case.
Nigerian newspapers are further limited by a shortage
of funds and by transportation difficulties. Oral
transmission of written material is a variable
difficult to measure, but could be substantial. The
need for further research is clearly indicated.

159. COKER, Increase. "Government Sponsors the
Competition," IPI Report, 1968, pp. 16-17.
An examination of the history of the press. The author
also discusses three types of media ownership and
control, and attempts to explain the involvement of the
government in press ownership.

160. COKER, Increase. Seventy Years of the Nigerian
Press. Lagos: Daily Times Limited, n. d.
A discussion of the history of some of the major
Nigerian newspapers, including national, regional,
provincial weekly, religious, vernacular and trade
publications. Newspaper style before 1926 is also
discussed. Newspaper professional practice,
particularly in the Daily Times, is specially
mentioned.

161. COKER, H.E. Landmarks of the Nigerian Press.
Lagos: National Press Ltd., 1970.
One of the most frequently referenced works on the
history of Nigerian press and the development of press
laws during the colonial period. This book also
contains information on the provisions of the early
press laws, and attempts to examine the roots of those
laws. For example, the author contends that the
Official Secrets Ordinance No.2 of 1841 was an
adaptation of the Official Secrets Act of the United
Kingdom.

162. COLEMAN, James S. Nationalism in Nigeria. Ph.D
dissertation, Harvard University, 1953.
An examination of the movement for nationalism in
Nigeria. The role of the newspaper as a revolutionary
weapon in the struggle for political independence is
described. This study has been published in a revised
form as Nigeria: Background to Nationalism. Berkeley,
California: University of California Press, 1958.

163. COLEMAN, James. Nigeria: Background to
Nationalism. Berkeley: University of California Press,
1958.

Among other things, author writes about the
revolutionary role of the press during the fight
against British imperial rule and colonial domination.
A major point stressed is that there can be little
doubt that nationalist newspapers and pamphlets were
among the main influences in awakening racial and
political consciousness in Nigeria before independence
in 1960.

164. COLEMAN, James S. "The Politics of Sub-Saharan
Africa," In Gabriel A. Almond & James S. Coleman
(Eds.), The Politics of Developing Areas. Princeton,
New Jersey: Princeton University Press, 1960.
Author looks at the politics of African countries south
of the Sahara, with special focus on the development
and function of the press in the region. The point is
made that the press in Nigeria was the principal medium
of agitational politics, and the recruitment of most
literate Africans into the political arena as well as
for the inculcation of nationalist sentiments. Some
leading newspapers, including the Daily Times and
Azikiwe's chain of newspapers are mentioned.

165. COLEMAN, James S. "Nationalism in Tropical
Africa," In William John Hanna (Ed.), Independent Black
Africa: The Politics of Freedom. Chicago: Rand McNally
and Company, 1964.
An analysis of the rise of nationalism in tropical
Africa, and the role of the press in the political
movements that ushered in independence for the states
of that region, including Nigeria. Author notes that
the most potent instrument used in the propagation of
nationalist ideas and racial consciousness has been the
indigenous press. Mention is made of the Nigerian
press, particularly the involvement of the press in
nationalism.

166. COLLE, Royal D. (Ed.), Perspectives on Mass Media
Systems. New York: Cornell University, 1968.
Among other things, this book provides information
based on a study of broadcasting in Nigeria.

167. CONOVER, Helen F. Africa South of the Sahara: A
Selected, Annotated List of Writings. Washington, D.C.:
Library of Congress, 1963.
An annotated bibliography of some of the major
publications on African countries south of the Sahara,
including Nigeria. It provides a list of some of the
works that among other things, describe the role of the
Nigerian press in the movement for nationalism.

An Annotated Bibliography

168. CROWDER, Michael. <u>A Short History of Nigeria</u>.
New York: Frederick A. Praeger, 1962.
Contains information on the role of the press and the
rise of Nigerian nationalism. Specific mention is made
of the names of newspapers, and their editors with
respect to their ceaseless attacks on the colonial
government.

169. DARKUP, Veronica P.S. "An Historical Overview of
the Development of the Nigerian Mass media: Newspaper,
Radio and Television." M.S. thesis, University of
kansas, 1981.
This thesis traces the development of mass media of
communication in Nigeria, the missionary press,
magazine, government information departments, radio and
television. Press freedom is also examined vis-avis
federal regulations, regional newspaper laws and the
Nigerian Press Council Decree of 1978.

170. DAMA, Na'ankot P.D. "The Development of
Broadcasting in Nigeria: Political and technical
problems, 1932-1982." M.S. thesis, Iowa State
University, 1982.
This study looks at the development of broadcasting in
the context of Nigeria's political changes. The author
contends that the history of the evolution of Nigerian
broadcasting is one greatly affected by political
developments. Some problems facing the industry are
mentioned, and recommendations on how the industry's
output might be improved are also made.

171. DARAMOLA, Abayomi C. <u>The Role of Communication
in Economic and Social Development in the Less
Developed Countries With Particular Reference to Family
Planning in Nigeria</u>. Ph. d dissertation, University of
Illinois at Urbana-Champaign, 1982.
This study examines the role of communication in the
socio-economic development of less developed countries
in general and Nigeria in particular. The role of the
press is to inform people about population constraints
to economic and social development and to motivate them
to practice birth control.

172. DARE, O.D. <u>Military Leadership and Political
Development in the Western State of Nigeria</u>. Ph.D
dissertation, Carleton University, Ottawa, Ontario,
Canada, 1972.
Examines military leadership and political development
in the former western state. How did this development
affect the press? The author notes that in addition to
economic difficulties which restricted newspaper
circulation in the state, the military government's

37

over-sensitivity created more difficulties for
journalists. As a result, the press was unable to
provide the vital communication link uniting the
government and the governed.

173. DARE, Olatunji. The News Agency of Nigeria: A
Study of Its Impact on the Flow of News and Role
Conceptions of Its Staffers. Ph.D dissertation, Indiana
University, 1983.
Author examines the role of the News Agency of Nigeria
(NAN) in the flow of news to, from and within Nigeria,
and the role conception of its staffers. The study
concludes that NAN does not emphasize news of
development over news of conflict, crime and disasters.
Reporting is focused on events rather than on process.
NAN relies on AP, Reuters and AFP for the bulk of its
foreign news. Domestic news is mainly from the
national and state capitals. For NAN staffers who see
themselves as educators, social engineers and public
watchdogs, inability to carry out more than routine
newsgathering is a source of frustration.

174. DAURA, Mamman. "Editing a Government Newspaper
in Nigeria," In Olav Stokke (Ed.), Reporting Africa.
New York: African Publishing Corporation, 1977.
Press freedom in Nigeria is not born out of government
wish or preference but out of the pluralist nature of
the society.

175. DAVIDSON, Basil. "The African Challenge," Index
on Censorship, vol. 13, no. 1, 1984, p. 2.
A panorama of the press in Africa. Mention is made of
Nigerian press. In the colonial period, Nigeria was
not without interesting newspapers. Post independence
Nigeria, even by 1967, had no fewer than eighteen
dailies, fifteen weeklies and twenty-two periodicals
that have "enjoyed a wide measure of freedom of
comment, as well as safeguards against persecution." A
casual contrast is made between press freedom in
Nigeria and Mozambique.

176. DAVIS, Burl E. System Variables and Agricultural
Innovativeness in Eastern Nigeria. Ph.D dissertation,
Michigan State University, 1968.
A study of diffusion of information. The author
explores the relations between individual modernizing
characteristics of Nigerian farmers, the corresponding
systems characteristics and the individual's
innovativeness. Eighteen communities in the former
Eastern region of Nigeria are studied.

177. DAVIS, Morris. <u>Interpreters For Nigeria: The Third World and International Public Relations</u>. Urbana, Illinois: University of Illinois Press, 1977. What public relations efforts did the Federal Military Government of Nigeria make to win international goodwill and understanding of its side of the story of the Nigerian civil crisis (1967-1970)? Did the secessionist rebel enclave led by Chukwuemeka Ojukwu make any efforts in that direction also? The author argues that the Nigerian government was sloppy in its international public relations efforts. Numerous examples of inefficient handling of crucial information by the Federal Military Government are given.

178. DE-GOSHIE, Joe. <u>Mass Media and National Development: A Content Analysis of a Nigerian Developmental Television Drama Series</u> --"Cock Crow at Dawn." Ph.D dissertation, Ohio University, 1985. This study attempts to describe and measure the type and amount of development themes contained in "Cock Crow at Dawn," a Nigerian television drama series designed to support the country's agricultural development. The study reveals that in spite of the declared objectives of both the government and the television authorities, the drama series contained more non-agricultural themes. Themes relating to agriculture ranked third among eleven content categories. The study tends to warn that creating a developmental communication program without appropriate organizational structure can greatly hamper the attainment of program objectives.

179. DEUTSCH, Richard, "The Nigerian Example," <u>Africa Report</u>, vol. 24, no. 4, 1979, pp. 46-51. The drafters of the 1979 Constitution balked at giving complete freedom to the press, which is required to support the Constitution and the rule of law. References are also made to the role of the press in national development, Nigerian press council, national news agency, broadcasting stations, daily and weekly newspapers.

180. DIAMON, Larry. "Nigeria: High Stakes for Babangida," <u>Africa Report</u>, vol. 30, no.6, 1985, pp. 54-57. This article looks at the Ibrahim Babangida regime vis-a-vis the mountain of socio-economic difficulties of Nigeria. Reference is made to Muhammadu Buhari's dealings with the press. According to the author, Buhari shackled the vigorously independent and increasingly sophisticated press, utilizing Decree No. 4 of 1984 -- Public Officers (Protection Against False

Accusation) Decree. This repression not only offended
a national tradition of free criticism and open debate,
but also cut off the regime from the growing
disaffection with its policies and style of rule.
Reference is made to Babangida's relationship with the
press which the author sees as more cordial than
Buhari's.

181. DIAMOND, Leslie A. W. "Bringing Radio and
Television to Northern Nigeria." EBU Review, no. 93b,
September 1965, pp. 27-29.
A detailed account of the steps taken to establish the
Broadcasting Company of Northern Nigeria Ltd., the BCNN
Ltd., or Radio Kaduna which went on air at 3 p.m. on
March 15, 1962, the anniversary of self-government in
Northern Nigeria.

182. DODSON, Don C. Onitsha Pamphlets: Culture in
the Marketplace. Ph.D dissertation, University of
Wisconsin, Madison, 1974.
This study traces the historical development and
structure of pamphleteering in Onitsha, a major
entrepot in Nigeria. The immediate roots of the
pamphlets lay in the 1940's when pamphlets by Nigerian
authors began to appear in such cities as Aba and
Lagos. The civil war interrupted their development;
but by 1971 after the end of hostilities,
pamphleteering had revived on a smaller scale. The
pamphlets, often referred to as "Onitsha market
literature," include love stories, handbooks of advice
and political drama.

183. DODSON, Don and Barbara Dodson. "Publishing
Progress in Nigeria." Scholarly Publishing, vol. 4, no.
1, 1972, pp. 61-72.
A discussion of the emergence of the Nwankwo-Ifejika
Company, a native publisher in Nigeria. The market it
hopes to cater to is described and analyzed in some
detail. The initial work and problems they have faced
are enumerated.

184. DODSON, Don & william A. Hachten. "Communication
and Development: African and Afro-American Parallels,"
Journalism Monographs, no. 28, 1973, pp. 1-37.
A revised version of a paper presented to the
International Communication Division of the AEJ
conference in Columbia, South Carolina in August 1971,
this paper attempts to draw analogies between
communication patterns among Africans and African-
Americans in the United States. Information on mass
media exposure, media preferences and communication
habits in Nigeria are provided.

185. DOGHUDJE, C. A. "The Department of Journalism of the University of Nigeria, Nsukka," Gazette, vol. 11, no. 4, 1964, pp. 329-330.
This article looks at journalism education in Nigeria, and especially focuses on journalism degree program at the University of Nigeria, Nsukka, the country's premier journalism degree program. Three of the five objectives of the department are highlighted. The syllabus is described, and an international award to the weekly student newspaper, The Record, is mentioned.

186. DOMATOB, Jerry K. "Propaganda Techniques in Black Africa," Gazette, vol. 36, no. 3, 1985, pp. 193-212.
An examination of the use of conventional propaganda techniques -- name calling, glittering generality, transfer, plain folks, testimonial, bandwagon, card-stacking etc -- in Africa. The study provides useful examples of how these techniques have been used in the Nigerian press by the country's top political figures, including Shehu Shagari, Muhammadu Buhari, Chukwuemeka Odumegwu Ojukwu, Nnamdi Azikiwe, and Yakubu Gowon.

187. DOMATOB, Jerry K., & Stephen W. Hall, "Development Journalism in Black Africa," Gazette, vol. 31, no. 1, 1983, pp. 9-33.
A review of the evolving context of development journalism, the various rationales and rhetoric attached to the concept as well as its current status. Nigeria is frequently mentioned, and useful pieces of information on some newspapers, journalists, media ownership and professional practice are provided.

188. DOOB, Leonard W. Communication in Africa: A Search for Boundaries. New Heaven, Connecticut: Yale University Press, 1966.
Although this book specifically deals with communications in Africa, it presents useful information on several aspects of mass communication that should be useful to scholars of Nigerian press.

189. DRAYTON, Arthur, "Educational Broadcasting in Nigeria: A Critique," Nigerian Opinion, vol. 1, no. 4, 1965, pp. 9-11.
The failure of the nation's broadcasting industry to assign top priority to education is the subject examined in this article. Western Nigerian Television (WNTV) which was originally conceived as an educational channel, has regrettably not lived up to expectations as an educational channel. The main conclusion is that the nation's broadcasting must depart from the Anglo-American model; it should be utilized to address

Nigeria's educational needs. The author makes
suggestions on how this can be achieved.

190. EBIWARE, Joseph M. Planning and Development of an
Educational Television System For Adult Education in
Nigeria. Ph.D dissertation, Syracuse University, 1986.
Based on a survey of forty-four high-ranking government
officials and local opinion leaders, this study
formulates a draft model plan for an educational
television system for adult education in Nigeria. The
author argues that adult education is crucial in a
country's socio-political and economic development.

191. ECHERUO, Michael J.C. "Developments in the
Nigerian Press 1960-1971." Nigerian magazine, nos. 110-
112, 1974, pp. 50-61.
A discussion of some of the changes in Nigerian press
from 1960 to 1971 such as changes in technical quality,
sales and advertisement as well as management. The
article also looks at the death of the national dailies
of the early times, the rise of the columnist, the
quality of magazines and the decline of radio-
television journalism.

192. EDEANI, David O. "The Impact of Government
Participation on the African Press." M.A. thesis,
University of Wisconsin, 1971.
This study looks at the effect of government ownership
of the mass media in Africa. The study shows that
between 1960 and 1970 government ownership of the media
grew steadily while private ownership increased up to
1966. It provides background on which information
about Nigerian press can be found.

193. EDEANI, David O. "Ownership and Control of the
Press in Africa." Gazette. vol. 16, no. 1, 1970, pp.
55-66.
An examination of ownership and control patterns of the
press in Africa. However, it provides some background
on Nigerian press both from historical and
philosophical points of view. The author believes that
mass media in private hands in Africa, including
Nigeria, could fail to serve the public interest,
especially in a developing society unfamiliar with the
intricacies of modern democracy.

194. EDEANI, David O. "West African Mass
Communication Research at Major Turning Point."
Gazette, Vol. 41, no. 3, 1988, pp. 149-183.
This study is an attempt to review critically mass
communication research in West Africa. It examines the
trend of mass communication research especially from

the 1960's, and evaluates the kinds of phenomena
studied, the research methodologies utilized, the kinds
of researchers involved and the quality of the research
studies produced. In addition, the author examines the
path that present West African communication should be
taking now and in the future.

195. EDOGA-UGWUOJU, Dympna, "Ownership Patterns of
Nigerian Newspapers," Gazette, vol. 33, no. 3, 1984,
pp. 193-201.
This work identifies two ownership patterns in the
Nigerian press, government and private. The latter is
broken into the following categories: individual
media, political party and missionary ownership. This
has been the pattern of newspaper ownership in Nigeria
since independence in 1960, and still remains that way.

196. EGBOH, Edmund O. "Industrial Relations and the
Press in Nigeria." Civilizations (Belgium), vol. 20,
no. 4, 1970, pp. 541-553.
The press in Nigeria started to concern itself actively
with industrial relations affairs during World War II.
The sympathy of the press was aroused by the hardships
which the workers suffered because of increases in the
cost of living without a comparable rise in wages. The
West African Pilot in particular constantly urged
improvements in the hours, wages and working conditions
of the workers and the improvement of trade unions.
The press supplied the moral support, encouragement,
and inspiration which the working class needed to
obtain better treatment.

197. EGBON, Michael I. The Origin and Development of
Television Broadcasting in Nigeria: An Inquiry into
Television Development in a Non-Industrialized Nation.
Ph.D dissertation, The University of Wisconsin -
Madison, 1977.
This dissertation is another scholarly effort to study
the background, development and status of television
broadcasting in Nigeria. It focuses on the development
of Nigerian television service from 1959 to 1977. The
research traces government involvement in television
industry, policy formation, organizational structure,
and major programming patterns during the evolution of
Nigeria's post-independence television service.

198. EGBON, Mike. "Federal Television Service and the
Issue of National Development and Unity in Nigeria,"
Gazette, vol. 29, no. 3, 1982, pp. 179-188.
Examines the federal government policy and rationale
for taking over Nigerian television. Some of the
lapses and possible abuses in the new Nigerian

Television Authority structure as well as problems of growth in the television system are highlighted. The problems of technological infrastructure and the paucity of television receiver sets are specially mentioned. Author tends to argue that totalitarianism, more than any other factor, was the main driving force behind the federal government takeover of the television industry.

199. EGBON, Mike. "Western Nigeria Television Service: Oldest in Tropical Africa" Journalism quarterly, vol. 60, no. 2, 1983, pp. 329-334. Author evaluates the historical development of tropical Africa's first television service - WNTV - as a total process within the sociopolitical context of western Nigeria.

200. EKWELIE, Sylvanus A. "The Nigerian Press Under Military Rule," Gazette, vol. 25, no. 4, 1979, pp. 219-232. When the military assumed control of Nigeria in 1966, there were a number of laws already regulating the mass media. However, the three military governments of 1966-79 did not attempt to exercise any censorship powers strenuously. There were cases of harassment and detention of newsmen but throughout that period, the media continued to enjoy some freedom. The Nigerian military governments displayed much the same appreciation for and fear of a free press as other governments.

201. EKWELIE, Sylvanus A. The Press in Gold Coast Nationalism, 1880-1957. Ph.D dissertation, The University of Wisconsin, 1971. Although this study focuses on the Ghanaian press and the nationalist movement, it provides valuable information on the West African press and Nigerian press. For example, the author notes that the story of the press in Nigeria is not only similar to that of the Gold Coast but is also an embodiment of the nationalist spirit and a response to a set of phenomena created by the colonial situation.

202. EKWELIE, Sylvanus A. "The content of Broadcasting in Nigeria." M.A. thesis, University of Wisconsin, 1968. The main purpose of the study is 1) to delineate the objectives of the broadcast media in Nigeria, and 2) to determine their percentage time allocation to various program contents. The study concludes that both radio and television are principally entertainment media because entertainment is found to have the lion's share

of all programming while news-information and education
follow in that order.

203. EKWELIE, Sylvanus A. "National Development and
Mass Communication Education: A Nigerian Profile," In
L. Erwin Atwood, Stuart J. Bullion and Sharon M. Murphy
(Eds.), International Perspectives on News (pp. 159-
166). Carbondale, Illinois: Southern Illinois
University Press, 1982.
The author argues that it takes education and
discipline to report, write and produce media programs
that can contribute toward national development. In
this respect, the universities offering mass
communication degree programs need to evaluate the
contributions of media toward national development.

204. EKWELIE, Sylvanus A. "The Nigerian Press Under
Civilian Rule," Journalism Quarterly, vol. 63, no. 1,
1986, pp. 98-104, 149.
The major premise of this study is that constitutional
provisions may be a necessary but not a sufficient
condition for the existence of a free press. An
additional premise is that Nigeria's ethnic cleavages,
political pluralism and occasional judicial activism
appear to provide a stronger bulwark against press
harassment than statutory guarantees. The major
conclusion of this study of press freedom under the
Shehu Shagari civilian rule (1979-1983), is that the
press escaped serious mauling in spite of political and
human frailties. Thanks, however, to the 1979
Constitution and Nigeria's independent courts.

205. EKWENSI, Cyprain. Broadcasting and Television in
West Africa. Liverpool: John Holt, 1961.
The author, a successful novelist, and former high
official in the Nigerian Ministry of Information,
focuses on broadcasting in West Africa. Valuable
information on Nigerian broadcasting is provided.

206. ELIAS, T.O. Nigerian Press law. Lagos: Evans
Brothers Ltd., 1969.
A very authoritative and often-referenced source on
Nigerian press law. The author, university law
professor and former Federal Attorney General describes
the historical developments and provisions of Nigerian
press laws.

207. ELIAS, T.O. "The Contribution of
Telecommunications and Direct Satellite Broadcasting to
Technical Assistance and Nation-Building in the `New'
Countries: An African Viewpoint," In Edward McWhinney

(Ed.), <u>The International Law of Communications</u> (pp. 122-137). New York: Oceana Publications Inc., 1971.
The author looks at the contribution of telecommunications and direct satellite broadcasting in the Third World with special focus on Africa, and Nigeria particularly. Information on the development of telecommunication and satellite in Nigeria is provided along with Nigeria's relationship with other countries in this field.

208. ENAHORO, Peter. "Africa -- The press in a One Party State." Paper presented at the International Press Institute Assembly, London, May 25-27, 1965.
A veteran Nigerian journalist talks of the press in Africa, and seems to argue that one-party government is antithetical to the ideals of freedom of the press.

209. ENAHORO, Peter. <u>Fugitive Offender: The Study of a Political Poisoner</u>. London: Cassel and Company Ltd., 1965.
Provides insights to press criticisms of British colonial policies. For example, the author makes the point that the editorial policy of one of the <u>West African Pilot's</u> sister newspapers -- the <u>Southern Nigerian Defender</u> -- was to arouse political consciousness among the people, to expose petty tyrannies, inefficiencies and mistakes of British officials, and to agitate for more by Nigerians in the administration, the appointment of Nigerians to higher positions in public service, and parity of treatment with expatriate officials.

210. ENAHORO, Peter, "Africa's Besieged Press," <u>Africa</u>, no. 21 (May), 1973.
A discussion of the problems of freedom of the press and censorship in African countries that also provides some information on the press in Nigeria.

211. EPELLE, Sam. "Communicating with the New Africa." <u>Communique</u>, no. 8 (February), 1967, pp. 8-13.
A Nigerian public relations practitioner discusses the professional communicator's role in African society, including Nigeria, and the important variables that influence the role of the communicator.

212. ESEMA, Ibok D. "Steps in the Development of the Press as a Mass Communication Medium in Nigeria," M.A. thesis, Temple University, 1968.
Author's focus is on developing the press as a mass communication medium in Nigeria.

213. Europa Yearbook 1986: A World Survey vol II.
London: Europa Publications Limited, 1986.
First published in 1926 and began to appear in annual
two-volume editions since 1960, The Europa yearbook has
become established as an authoritative reference work,
providing a wealth of detailed information on socio-
political and economic institutions of the world,
including the press. Very useful information is
provided on Nigerian press: daily, weekly and Sunday
newspapers, English language magazines and other
periodicals, news agency, publishers, radio and
television.

214. EWELUKWA, Dennis I.D. Freedom of Political
Expression in the United States, India and Nigeria.
Ph.D dissertation, Yale University, 1966.
A cross-national study of freedom of political
expression in three different political entities:
United States of America, India and Nigeria.

215. EZEOKOLI, Victoria. "Challenges of Programme
Production In Nigerian Television, Combroad, no. 69,
1985, pp. 20-22.
Author examines some of the problems and challenges of
program production in Nigerian Television Authority
(NTA). Most serious among the problems are
insufficient funds and minimal production equipment.
NTA's efforts vis-a-vis these challenges are mentioned,
and they have paid off. A casual comparison is also
made between program production in Nigeria and Great
Britain. The author provides valuable statistical data
on NTA programming and broadcasting hours.

216. EZEOKOLI, Victoria. "Television For Development
in Nigeria." Combroad, December 1988, pp. 16-18.
A review of the role of Nigerian television in the
country's development efforts. The author, who is the
director of programs at the Nigerian Television
Authority, Lagos, highlights some of the successes of
television in promoting agricultural and health
programs. However, the Nigerian television is still
very far from attaining its full potential in the
deliberate and structured use of broadcasting for the
pursuit and attainment of development goals, the author
argues. The main conclusion is that it is necessary
for program producers to work in close liaison with
health workers and for both parties to constantly
update their knowledge.

217. EZERA, K. Constitutional Developments in Nigeria.
London: Cambridge university Press, 1964.

This work's focus is on the history and constitutional development of Nigeria. However, it provides information on the role of the press in that process. For example, the author notes that the press played a tremendous part in agitating for constitutional reforms and increased self-government, and in molding public opinion against British colonial policies in the country.

218. FAGEN, richard R, "Relation of Communication Growth to National Political Systems in the Less Developed Countries," Journalism Quarterly, vol. 41, no. 1, 1964, pp. 87-94.
A Study of communication in fifty nations, including Nigeria. The main conclusion of the study is that a country may grow rapidly in either the newspaper or radio sector of mass media without necessarily enjoying a similar growth in the other.

219. FARACE, Vincent & Lewis Donohew, "Mass Communication in National Social Systems: A Study of 43 Variables in 115 countries," Journalism Quarterly, vol. 42, no. 2, 1965, pp. 253-261.
A cross-cultural study of press freedom in 117 countries, including Nigeria. Through a regression analysis, authors develop a set of eight "predictors" which seem to be of particular importance in relation to the level of a country's communication system, including press freedom.

220. FARACE, Vince, "A Study of Mass Communication and National Development," Journalism Quarterly, vol. 43, no. 2, 1966, pp. 305-313.
A study of fifty-four variables in one hundred, nine countries reveals that media development in those countries, including Nigeria, is closely related to many aspects of a country's development, and a national development continuum underlies correlations among those variables, studied.

221. FASHINA, O. "Radio Progress and Plans." E.B.U. Review, no. 71, January 1962, pp. 27-28.
Reports on the progress of the Nigerian Broadcasting Corporation and a five-year development plan for 1962-1967.

222. FASHINA, O. "School Broadcasting and Other Developments." E.B.U. Review, no. 72b, March 1962, pp. 32-33.
A report on some positive developments in the Nigerian Broadcasting Corporation such as the commencement of

the school broadcasting unit and commercial
advertisements.

223. FIOFORI, Ferdinand O. The Role of Oral Narratives
in Dissemination of Family Planning Information in
Rural Africa. Ph.D dissertation, University of Colorado
at Boulder, 1978.
This study tests the effectiveness of traditional means
of communication to diffuse information in areas where
mass media are not consumed extensively, including
rural areas of Nigeria. The results suggest that by
refining and using a traditional communication medium
such as oral narratives which are a quotidian part of
rural people's experience, a topology of an information
unit accessible to every household in rural Africa can
be constructed. Thus, instead of waiting for a future
time when modern mass media fare could be available to
every household in rural Africa before adequately
giving them developmental information, the traditional
communication modes already available in these areas
should be utilized for dissemination of innovative
developmental messages.

224. FISCHER, Heinz-Dietrich & John C. Merrill (eds.),
International Communication: Media, Channels,
Functions. New York: Hastings House Publisher, 1970.
A collection of several articles on international
communication, covering numerous aspects of mass
communication in many countries. Scanty but useful
information on rural press, cinema and educational
broadcasting in Nigeria is provided.

225. FLINT, John E. Nigeria and Ghana. Englewood
Cliffs, New Jersey: Prentice-Hall, Inc., 1966.
Although this book describes the histories of Nigeria
and Ghana, it provides information that could be useful
to Nigerian journalism historians. For example, it
provides some background information about the pioneer
newspaper entrepreneurs in West Africa. Mention is also
made of Nnamdi Azikiwe's journalistic career and the
West African Pilot, the leading Nigerian organ of
nationalist opinion during the struggle against British
colonialism.

226. FOLORUNSO, Isola. "FRCN Zonal Structure in
Nigeria: A New Dimension in Radio Broadcasting,"
Combroad, no. 46, 1980, pp. 12-13.
A description of some of the functions of the Federal
Radio Corporation of Nigeria, and the zonal structure
of the corporation which brought in new dimensions in
radio broadcasting. Some problems and prospects of
radio broadcasting in the country are discussed.

227. FOLORUNSO, Isola. "Grassroots Broadcasting in
Nigeria," Combroad, no. 60, 1983, pp. 7-9.
An examination of the historical background of the
development and evolution of sound (radio) broadcasting
in Nigeria with special emphasis on the major
milestones that occurred in the process. The author
argues that the revolution in "grassroots broadcasting"
began in 1967 with the advent of military rule in the
country, and the creation of twelve states from the
former regions of the country.

228. FOLORUNSO, Isola. "Radio Broadcasting in Multi-
Lingual Nigeria," Combroad, no. 67, 1985, pp. 5-8.
Multi-lingual broadcasting in Nigeria has been
effectively used to construct a solid infrastructure
for a peaceful, stable, self-reliant and dynamic
Nigerian society, and in addition, in the promotion of
literacy campaigns, environmental sanitation, social
education, health care education and civic duties. In
order to widen the scope of multi-lingual broadcasting,
the author suggests that developing countries,
including Nigeria, should make technological
innovations in the field of electronics and
telecommunications.

229. FROST, J.M. (Ed.), World Radio TV Handbook.
London: Billboard Publications, Inc., 1972.
A reference book on world radio and television.
Information is provided on Nigerian programming,
domestic and external broadcasting services as well as
federal and state radio/television stations.

230. FYLE, Clifford M. "The Production and Flow of
Books in Africa," In Books For the Developing
Countries: Asia, Africa. Paris: UNESCO, 1965.
Author's main focus is on the social aspects of level
of literacy and language difficulties as well as such
economic aspects as copyright, trade barriers and
materials in African countries, including Nigeria.

231. GOLDING, Peter & Philip Elliott. Making the
News. London: Longman, 1979.
Where does the bulk of the news content of Nigerian
broadcast media come from? Authors point out that 85%
of the news content of the Nigerian broadcast media
comes from the big transnational news agencies located
in Western Europe: Reuters, Associated Press, Agance
France Presse and the Visnews.

232. GALLGHER, Wes. "Odds Against Press Freedom in
Africa," Editor & Publisher, August 4, 1962.

A discussion on freedom of the press in Africa. The author contends that the press in Africa is engaged in a battle for freedom, but adds that in Nigeria, the press is free and vocal.

233. GRAETTINGER, Diana I. The Development of Broadcasting in the Former British West African Possessions of Sierra Leone, Ghana (the Gold Coast), Nigeria and the Gambia. Ph.D dissertation, Northwestern University, 1977.
An examination of the development of electronic mass media systems in the former British West African colonies of Sierra Leone, Ghana, Nigeria and the Gambia. The study also examines the parallel lines of influence, both cultural and historical, European and African, that have acted as `primary' and `secondary' influences in the development of broadcast systems in these four countries. The historical similarity of the development of broadcasting in the four countries is also provided.

234. GRAHAM & Gillies Publishers. Media Guide For Nigeria, Ghana, Liberia and Sierra leone. Accra, Ghana: Graham & Gillies, 1968.
Provides statistical data on broadcasting in four English-speaking West African countries -- Ghana, Liberia, Sierra Leone and Nigeria. Data is also provided on circulation of publications, movie theatres, radio listenership and cost of television commercials.

235. GRANT, Marcia A. "Nigerian Newspaper Types." Journal of Commonwealth Political Studies, vol. 9, no. 2, 1971, pp. 95-114.
Although Nigerian newspapers have the highest circulation in Africa, their effectiveness is limited by geographical, economic, social and political parochialism. Tribal loyalties provide the most difficult obstacle to overcome in the establishment of a truly national newspaper. Foreign-owned commercial papers tend to arouse anti-colonial resentment. Government and tribal organs are limited in effectiveness to their cores of supporters. Limited literacy and transportation difficulties act as additional barriers. Despite these problems, the press has generally survived internal disruptions, including the civil war as well as regional and political pressures.

236. GRANT, M.M. "Challenge to the New Government: The Press," Nigerian Opinion, vol. 2, no. 3, 1966, pp. 33-35.

A reflection on what the role of the press should be under the first military government. The author remarks that the governments of the First Republic made the mistake of having their newspapers do nothing but flatter them, and thus they lost public trust. The challenge to the military government under Maj. Gen. Aguiyi Ironsi was not only to use the press to explain government policy but also to give the press the freedom to report accurately. This article also highlights some of the economic problems of government newspapers prior to the premier coup d'etat in January 1966.

237. GREENE, Michael T. Sons of the Fathers: Four Nigerian Writers. Ph.D dissertation, State University of new york at Buffalo, 1979.
This study looks at four writers in Nigeria: Amos Totula, Cyprain Ekwensi, John Pepper Clark and Chinua Achebe, individuals whose works illustrate many of the representative themes, critical tendencies and literacy movements that have emerged during this development. Each of these writers has faced some problems with language and historical tradition, and the individual solutions they have provided have been major contributions to the development of a national literature that is distinctively Nigerian.

238. HACHTEN, William A. "The Press in a One-Party State: The Ivory Coast Under Houphouet," Journalism Quarterly, vol. 44, no. 1, 1967, pp. 107-113.
A casual comparison between the Ivorien and Nigerian press is made in this study which focuses on the authoritarian tradition of the press in Ivory Coast. Author states that while the development of the press in Ivory Coast has lagged behind, the press in Nigeria has developed with more newspapers and periodicals published by indigenous entrepreneurs since the British intrusion.

239. HACHTEN, William A. "The Training of African Journalists," Gazette, vol. 14, no. 2, 1968, pp. 101-110.
A description of journalism education for African media practitioners. Special focus is made on short term and permanent journalism training programs in Africa, including Nigeria. Journalism training for African journalists abroad is also examined. The author highlights the pros and cons of each of these programs, and provides an impressive list of permanent schools of journalism in Africa, including Nigeria's premier college of journalism at Nsukka.

An Annotated Bibliography

240. HACHTEN, William A. Muffled Drums: The News Media in Africa. Ames, Iowa: The Iowa State University Press, 1971.
A general overview of mass communication in Africa. Information on early newspapers in Nigeria, their involvement in politics and relations with government is provided. With regard to press freedom in Nigeria, a major point stressed is that the press (of 1960 to 1965) was in many ways a unique phenomenon for Africa: diverse, outspoken, competitive and irreverent. The Nigerian press, unlike the press elsewhere on the continent, was unfettered until the later half of the decade when freedom of expression was curtailed.

241. HACHTEN, William A. "Ghana's Press Under the N.R.C.: An Authoritarian Model For Africa," Journalism Quarterly, vol. 52, no. 3, 1975, pp. 458-464, 583.
Author contends that the authoritarian model of mass communication, as exemplified by the role of the Ghanaian press under the National Redemption Council -- NRC -- can be applied to any African media system, including a mass media system as diverse as Nigeria's. Nigeria is also mentioned as one of the African countries that have recognized the need for better on-the-job training, more short courses for working journalists and recruitment of university graduates as a step to raising the level of journalism.

242. HARE, A. Paul. "Cultural Differences in Performance in Communication Networks in Africa, the United States, and the Philippines," Sociology and Social Research, vol. 54, no. 1, 1969, pp. 25-41.
In a variation of the Leavitt communication network experiment, university students in Nigeria, the United States, South Africa, and the Philippines are compared in wheel and circle networks in four-man groups. The largest differences appear between the U.S groups and the Nigerian groups in the wheel, and the U.S. groups and the Philippine groups in the circle. With the exception of the Yoruba in Nigeria, all groups send fewer messages but take more time to solve the problems in the wheel than in the circle. Cultural differences appear to account for the differences in the behavior of the group members.

243. HARRIS, John R, "Nigerian Enterprise in the Printing Industry." Nigerian Journal of Economic and Social Studies, vol. 10, no. 2, 1968, pp. 215-227.
An evaluation of the printing industry as an enterprise in Nigeria. The structure of the printing industry, the prevalent indigenous printing firms as of 1965 and the funding and growth of the industry, are examined.

53

244. HASAN, Abul. "The Book in Multilingual
Countries." UNESCO Reports and Papers on Mass
Communication, no. 82, Paris, 1978.
A survey based on the proceeding of a symposium on the
publication of books in the various languages of
multilingual countries, including Nigeria. The report
notes that Nigeria, Ghana and to a lesser extent,
Sierra Leone, are the most active publishing countries
in West Africa. The report shows that the total number
of languages and dialects shared by more than 100
ethnic groups in Nigeria is between 350 and 400. It
concludes that African countries with such a
multiplicity of languages are faced with great
difficulty in printing and publishing books in those
languages. The problems of publishing in those
languages are also pointed out.

245. HAULE, John J. Press Controls in Colonial
Tanganyika and Post-Colonial Tanzania 1930-1967: A
Proposition For Research in African Journalism History.
Ph.D dissertation, Southern Illinois University, 1984.
This study contends that the nature of the relationship
between the governors and the governed in the colonial
and post-colonial periods in sub-Saharan Africa was
primarily an authoritarian one. It proposes an
authoritarian press model as the most appropriate way
to study the press history in the region. However, the
study distinguishes Nigerian press as relatively
libertarian in nature.

246. HEAD, Sydney W. (Ed.) Broadcasting in Africa: A
Continental Survey of Radio and Television.
Philadelphia: Temple University Press, 1974.
Provides useful information and statistical data on
various aspects of broadcasting in Africa, including
Nigeria. Among the subjects discussed on Nigeria are
internal broadcasting to Nigerian audiences,
international services from Western Europe, communist
sources and African nations, religious broadcasting and
bilateral foreign aid.

247. HEAD, Sydney W. "African Mass Communications:
Selected Information Sources." Journal of
Broadcasting, Vol. 20, no. 3, 1976, pp. 381-415.
A listing of 460 published and unpublished research
works on African mass communication. It lists
newspaper and magazines sources, government
publications and records as well as books and journal
articles on mass communication in over 50 African
countries, including Nigeria which has the most
entries.

An Annotated Bibliography

248. HEAD, Sydney W., & Lois Beck. Bibliography of
African Broadcasting: An Annotated Guide. Philadelphia:
School of Communications and Theater, Temple
University, 1974.
This work of bibliography lists 458 annotated sources -
- sometimes unannotated -- on broadcasting in Africa.
A few items are included for Nigeria. Some of the items
listed could also be useful in the general area of mass
communication other than broadcasting.

249. HENRY, Kathleen. "Using Radio to Promote Family
Planning in Sub-Saharan Africa." Paper presented at
the AEJMC, Portland, Oregon, July 1988.
A discussion of the role of radio in communicating
social development programs in sub-Saharan Africa.
Mention is made of the use of radio and folk media,
including the "Talking Drum," in family planning
programs in Nigeria.

250. HOFSTAD, David H. "Changing a Colonial Image:
Pet-Singers and a Dynamic Newspaper Feed Northern
Nigeria's Political Awareness." Africa Report, vol.
16, no. 7, 1971, pp. 28-31.
A description of the growing political awareness in
Northern Nigeria, manifested in recent songs with
meaningful lyrics and a newspaper, Gaskiya Ta Fi Kwabo,
concerned with contemporary issues and problems. The
article throws light on some of the contents of the
Gaskiya Ta Fi Kwabo (truth is worth more than a penny),
a vernacular newspaper that was primarily a propaganda
sheet to arouse support for the war against Adolf
Hitler.

251. HOPKINSON, Tom. "A New Age of Newspapers in
Africa," Gazette, vol. 14, no. 2, 1968, pp. 79-84.
Can press freedom survive in a one-party state? This
article is a description of the views of three well
respected Nigerian journalists as well as a few
journalists from other parts of Africa on the issue.
The Nigerian journalists are Peter Enahoro of the Daily
Times, Herbert Unegbu, editor of the West African Pilot
and Zrydz-Eyutchae, deputy editor of the Pilot.

252. HUMPHREYS, E. S. "The Free Press of Nigeria."
Quill, November 1960, pp. 17-22.
An appraisal of press freedom by the dawn of
independence in 1960. Author remarks that the press
was free - and vigorously so.

253. HUNT, Garry T., & Michael P. Seng, "The Private
Press vs. the Military: A Case Study of Journalistic
Confrontation in Nigeria." Paper presented at the

International Communication Association (ICA)
conference in Montreal, Canada, May, 1987.
Authors examine the twenty months of Maj. Gen.
Muhammadu Buhari's military regime and the General's
efforts to control the private press. The main
conclusion is that the Buhari government greatly
threatened the press, rocking the very foundation of
its freedom. Clearly, while much threatened by Buhari,
the Nigerian press has emerged as strong as ever,
perhaps the strongest and most sophisticated press in
Africa.

254. HUNT, Gary T., & Michael P. Seng. "Government-
Press Relations in Nigeria: Conflict and Confrontation,
1880-1987." Paper presented at the annual meeting of
the AEJMC, Portland, Oregon, July 1988.
This paper traces the state of relations between the
press and the government over the century. Special
focus is made on Gen. Muhammadu Buhari's regime (1983-
1985) during which the status of an independent
Nigerian press was threatened by actions taken by the
government.

255. HURSH, Gerald D., Niels Rolling & Graham B. Kerr.
Innovation in Eastern Nigeria: Success and Failure of
Agricultural Programs in 71 Villages of Eastern
Nigeria. Diffusion of Innovation Research Report, no.
8. East Lansing: Michigan State University, Department
of Communication, 1968.
This study's focus is on diffusion of new agricultural
information to rural farmers in seventy-one villages in
Eastern Nigeria. A similar work was done later by
Joseph Ascroft.

256. HUTZELL, Richard W. "An Examination of the New
World Information Order." M.S. thesis, University of
Tennessee, Knoxville, 1983.
A content analysis of three major Nigerian newspapers
aimed at verifying or disproving charges that
developing countries are awash in a flood of
information, particularly from the western industrial
nations. The main conclusion is that Nigerian
newspapers do not reprint automatically the information
circulated by the Western news sources.

257. HYDLE, L.H. The Press and Politics in Nigeria.
Ph.D dissertation, Columbia University, 1972.
An analysis of the role of the press in the political
development, particularly in the movement for
nationalism. The author argues that the press itself
had played an important and honorable part in the
nationalist movement, and had come to be regarded as an

essential weapon in the armory of any serious political
party or movement. Brief comments on some newspaper
laws are also made.

258.   IDEMILI, Samuel. O. The West African Pilot and
the Movement For Nigerian Nationalism, 1937-1960. Ph.D
dissertation, University of Wisconsin, 1980.
This study examines the revolutionary activities of the
West African Pilot, the newspaper in the forefront of
the last phase of Nigerian nationalism. It examines
how the paper was used as a revolutionary weapon by its
founder and editor, Dr. Nnamdi Azikiwe, in awakening
racial and political consciousness among the erstwhile
passive Nigerian public, and in fighting British
imperialism in the country.

259.   IDOWU, Sobowale A. "Nigerian Newspapers' Handling
of Important National Issues: Ownership as an Influence
in News Coverage." M.A. thesis, Syracuse University,
1976.
This study investigates the effect of newspaper
ownership on news coverage in Nigeria, using two events
- the Udoji awards, the report of a commission set up
to review the salaries of civil servants and the
university student crisis of 1975. The private papers
contained more unfavorable stories on the two events
than the government papers.

260.   IGWEBIKE, Clement C. "A Comparative Study of the
Mass Media Use Patterns of Nigerian Rural and Urban
Populations," M.A. thesis, University of Georgia, 1980.
The communication behaviors of the Nigerian rural and
urban populations is the focal point of this study.
Generally, high media users are found to be more
knowledgeable on current affairs than low users, and
urban residents more knowledgeable than the rural. The
author believes that these are important facts to be
considered in any plan for development communication.

261.   IHATOR, Augustine I. The Impact of the Second
World War on West African Press and Politics -- the
Case of Nigeria. Ph.D dissertation, Howard University,
1984.
This study examines the impact of World War II on
NIgerian press and politics. It describes the
technical and professional changes in Nigerian media,
and links the socio-political and economic
transformation of the Nigerian society to the war and
the press. The author contends that the European
demand for West African participation in the war effort
provided a favorable condition under which the
nationalist press agitated for rapid political progress

-- and independence. The author further contends that
the establishment of several publications by Nigerian
nationalists for the political education of the public
and British government's establishment of its own
publications, the <u>Mirror</u> Group, to counter
nationalists' media propaganda, helped change the
technical quality and the distribution network of West
African publications.

262.   IWANG, Mbuk J. "Twenty Years of Nigerian
Television: 1959-1979." M.A. thesis, North Texas State
University, 1981.
This study reviews the evolution of Nigerian
broadcasting from 1935 to 1979, with emphasis on the
development of Nigerian television broadcasting. The
study concludes that both the heterogeneity of Nigerian
society and the country's continued political unrest
pose a threat to either private or government ownership
of television stations.

263.   IWOWO, Thelma N. "Audience Perceptions of the
Attractiveness and Persuasiveness of Modern
(Television) and Traditional (Ajasco) Advertising
Systems in Lagos, Nigeria." M.A. thesis, Cornell
University, 1983.
A study of audience perception of the attractiveness
and persuasiveness of television and indigenous medium
of advertising, <u>Ajasco</u>. <u>Ajasco</u> parallels the old
American tradition of "snake oil" sales in some ways.
The main conclusion is that the majority of people
prefer television advertising to <u>Ajasco</u> advertising.

264.   JAKANDE, L. K.   "The Press and Military Rule," In
Oyeleye Oyediran (ed.), <u>Nigerian Government and
Politics Under Military Rule, 1966-1979</u> (pp. 110-123).
New York: St. Martin's press, 1979.
Author examines the performance of the press during the
first thirteen years of military rule, and attempts to
understand if the press was free during that period.
Details of actions taken by military authorities to
suppress the press are given. The main conclusion is
that the press managed to conserve its freedom of
expression through the most difficult period of its
history --an achievement of great historic significance
not only for Nigeria but also for the world press as a
whole.

265.   JONES, CLEMENT. "Mass Media Codes of Ethics and
Councils: A Comprehensive International Study on
Professional Standard." UNESCO Reports and Papers on
Mass Communication, no. 86, Paris, 1980.

An Annotated Bibliography

This report contains a code of professional conduct adopted by the Nigerian Union of Journalists at its fifth national convention held in Benin City in 1970. The first item of the code stipulates that: "It is the primary duty of a journalist to tell and adore the truth."

266. JONES-QUARTERLY, K.A.B. A Life of Azikiwe. Baltimore: Penguin Books, 1965.
The author, a Ghanaian journalism historian, describes the life and professional career of Dr. Nnamdi Azikiwe, founder of Nigeria's first successful chain of newspapers. The role of the West African Pilot, the main paper in the chain, is described in relation to the politics for independence.

267. JOSE, Babatunde. "Press Freedom In Africa." African Affairs, vol. 74, no. 296, 1975, pp. 255-262. An overview of press freedom in Africa in general and Nigeria in particular. In Nigeria, the tradition of a vigorous and virile press dates beyond the period of British colonial administration. Throughout Africa, no press enjoyed the kind of freedom that marked the Nigerian press during the period of military rule. Even the elected government of the first Republic was not as tolerant of the press as the military. However, pressmen had some sad moments.

268. JOSE, Babatunde. "Anti-Colonial Strategy Now Destructive," IPI Report, vol. 24, no. 8, 1975, pp. 9,11.
Should the African press, especially the Nigerian, press which was used as a weapon in the fight against colonial rule also be used today in a war against post-colonial African governments? These are some of the questions the chairman of the Daily Times of Nigeria attempts to answer in this article.

269. JULY, Robert W. The Origins of Modern African Thought: Is Development in West Africa During the Nineteenth and Twentieth Centuries. New York: Frederick A. Pareger, 1967.
Contains valuable information on the role of the press in the movement for nationalism, especially the activities of the militant newspaper editors such as John Payne Jackson, Thomas Horatio Jackson, Herbert Macauley and Sir Kitoyi Ajasa.

270. KATZ, Elihu, George Wedell, Michael Pilsworth and Dov Shinar. Broadcasting in the Third World: Promise and Performance. Cambridge, Massachusetts: Harvard University Press, 1977.

Although this book describes broadcasting systems in
the developing countries, it provides valuable
information on Nigerian broadcasting system: its
development, educational broadcasting, finance,
objectives and goals, policy as well as the Nigerian
Broadcasting Corporation (NBC) and the role of
broadcasting in national development.

271.   KEITH, Robert F.   Information and Modernization:
A Study of Eastern Nigerian Farmers.   Ph.D
dissertation, Michigan State University, 1968.
This study examines the role of information in
modernization, using agricultural farmers in Eastern
Nigeria as a case study. Among other things, the study
finds the farmer's attitudes towards modernization and
innovations to be related to both individual's levels
of information and innovativeness.

272.   KEITH, Robert F. et al.   "Mass Media Exposure and
Modernization Among Villagers in Three Developing
Countries: Toward Cross-Cultural Generalization." Mass
Communication and the Development of Nations. East
Lansing: Michigan State University, International
Communication Institute, 1966.
A cross-cultural study on diffusion of information.
Three developing countries -- Brazil, India and Nigeria
-- are compared.

273.   KINNER, Joseph G. The Study of the Origins,
Development and Role of Radio Broadcasting in Southern
Nigeria. Ph.D dissertation, University of California,
Los Angeles, 1979.
An examination of the origins, development and role of
radio broadcasting in Southern Nigeria between 1923-
1951. The origins, development and role of radio
broadcasting in Southern Nigeria at this period were
tied directly to technical, socio-economic, political
and cultural factors. World War II and its aftermath
played a dominant role in influencing both the
considerations and the rate of development and the role
of radio broadcasting as well.

274.   KITCHEN, Helen (ed.).   The Press in Africa.
Washington, D.C.: Ruth Sloan Associates, Inc., 1956.
Provides an overview of the press in twenty-three
African countries, including Nigeria. An attempt has
been made to list some of the newspapers printed in the
country before the dawn of independence. The author
believes that editorial content at the period was
lively, and concludes that with the improvement in
communications, three or four truly national newspapers

along with some strictly parochial publications are
bound to spring up.

275. KITTROSS, John. <u>A Bibliography of Thesis and
Dissertations in Broadcasting: 1920-1973</u>. Washington,
D.C.: Broadcasting Education Association, 1978.
This work contains 4,334 unannotated bibliography of
master's theses and doctoral dissertations written in
the field of broadcasting mostly in United States
universities between 1920 and 1973. Five items, four
master's theses and one doctoral dissertation on
broadcasting in Nigeria, are listed.

276. KNOTT, J.A.C. "Radio Nigeria's Three-Year Plan."
<u>West African Review</u>. December 1958.
A discussion of a three-year plan for the development
of radio broadcasting before the achievement of
political independence.

277. KOLADE, Christopher. "The Expansion of the
Nigerian Broadcasting Service." <u>Combroad</u>, October-
December 1975, pp. 30-34.
Author, Director-General of Nigeria's national radio
system describes major development plans in the
national radio broadcasting system.

278. KOLADE, Christopher. "Hagerstown and Nigeria
Cooperate in ETV Project." <u>NAEB Review</u>, vol. 24, no. 3,
1965, pp. 18-21.
Describes the contract between Nigeria and the
Washington County Board of Education (Hagerstown ETV
Project) Under which the former was to work with
Nigeria in seeking improvements in educational
broadcasting.

279. KOLADE, Christopher. "Radio and Television in
the Fight Against Illiteracy and in the Fundamental
Instruction of Adults." <u>E.B.U Review</u>, no. 88b,
November 1964, pp. 22-23.
Radio and television have unique role to play in the
fight against illiteracy and in fundamental education.
But the high expenditure involved, particularly in
setting up television is a barrier to the medium's use
in fighting illiteracy. Another barrier is the absence
of concerted efforts by various government departments
in different countries.

280. KOLADE, Christopher. "Anglophone West Africa:
Nigeria," In Sydney W. Head (Ed.), <u>Broadcasting in
Africa: A Continental Survey of Radio and Television</u>.
(pp. 78-89). Philadelphia: Temple University Press,
1974.

An examination of the federal and state broadcasting
systems with special reference to such themes as
control and structure, finance, technical facilities
and programs. Other aspects examined include
educational broadcasting, commercial broadcasting,
external radio service, audience relations and
training. A short history of broadcasting is also
provided. The author points toward the restructuring
of the system under a united broadcasting and
television authority in which control could be shared
between the federal and state governments.

281. KOLADE, Christopher. "The Nigerian Broadcaster
and His Audience," Combroad, no. 46, 1980, pp. 27-30.
A discussion of how the Nigerian broadcaster can be
sure that he or she always keeps faith with his
audience. The issue of freedom of the media is also
discussed. The author is optimistic that the day is
not too far off when Nigerians will be operating the
"full freedom of the media" instead of merely talking
about it.

282. KOPYTOFF, Jean H. A Preface to Modern Nigeria.
Madison, Wisconsin: The University of Wisconsin Press,
1965.
Provides a brief history of Lagos press in the early
colonial period. Specific information is provided on
the voices of political protests in the press during
that period of Nigerian journalism history.

283. KURIAN, George T. (Ed.). World Press
Encyclopedia Vol. II. New York: Facts on File Inc.,
1982.
Provides a short but almost complete overview of
Nigerian press. Historical development of the press is
presented. Other aspects of the press covered include
pattern of ownership, economic framework of the press,
press laws and censorship, state-press relations,
attitude toward foreign media, education and training
opportunities for Nigerian journalists.

284. LADELE, Olu. "History of the Nigerian
Broadcasting Corporation," Combroad, no. 39, 1978, pp.
52-53.
A discussion of the history and development of
broadcasting in Nigeria, particularly after the coming
into existence of the Nigerian Broadcasting Corporation
(NBC) on April 1, 1957. The author contends that the
history of the corporation coincides in the main, with
the history of broadcasting in the country. State
government-owned stations which were established

An Annotated Bibliography

between 1959 and 1962 had different orientation from
the NBC.

285. LADELE, Olu, V. Olufemi Adefela & Olu Lasekan.
History of the Nigerian Broadcasting Corporation.
Ibadan: Ibadan University Press, 1979.
An in-depth discussion of the history of broadcasting
in Nigeria with special focus on the twenty-year-
history and development of the Nigerian Broadcasting
Corporation. Some of the problems facing the
broadcasting industry's future course are examined.

286. LARSON, Charles R. "New Writers, New Readers."
Wilson Quarterly, vol. 4, no. 1, 1980, pp. 81-92.
In this article, the author provides a sample of
Nigeria's world class literature, with an overview of
the country's publishing industry. The author contends
that the writing of fiction in sub-Sahara Africa in the
past twenty-five to thirty years, has been dominated by
Nigerian journalists, and by world standards, Nigerian
writers have been successful.

287. LEE, Paul S. National Communication and
Development: A Comparative Study of Four British
Colonies - Nigeria, Guyana, Singapore and Hong Kong.
Ph. D dissertation, The University of Michigan, 1986.
Examines the roles of mass media in the process of
national development in Nigeria, Guyana, Singapore and
hong Kong. Author contends that a better integration
of the societies of Singapore and Hong Kong is one
explanation for the faster rate of development there,
and mass communication is thought to play a part in the
process of integration. The media in the two countries
are participating in nation-building by de-emphasizing
socially disruptive issues of class and ethnicity.

288. LEGUM, Colin. "The Press in West Africa." IPI
Report, vol. 5, no. 11, 1957, pp. 1-3.
This article examines the press in the former British
colonies in West Africa. The trend towards self-
government and independence in these countries,
including Nigeria was strongly reflected both in the
policy and in the growth of the press. There was a
healthier atmosphere for successful newspaper
enterprise in Nigeria than in the other countries.
Information on the earliest newspapers in Nigeria such
as statistics on the number of papers and monthly
journals and circulation figures is given.

289. LINDFORS, Bernth. "The African Politician's
Changing Image in African Literature in English," The
Journal of Developing Areas, no. 4, 1969, pp. 13-28.

63

Using Nigerian English language works, the author
presents evidence to support the view that the image of
the African politician, as displayed through literature
in English, changes drastically after independence,
that the idealistic, self-sacrificing nationalist is
transformed into a greedy, self-seeking opportunist.

290. LINDFORS, Bernth. "The Early Writings of Wole
Soyinka," Journal of African Studies, vol. 2, no. 1,
1975, pp. 64-86.
A survey of the early literary career of Nigerian
author Wole Soyinka. It also provides in part, a
profile of Wole Soyinka who began his literary career
in the secondary school.

291. LLOYD, Nigel. Newspaper and the Law. Lagos:
Amalgamated Press, 1967.
A valuable reference book on press law.

292. MACEBUH, Stanley. "A Glaring Example of the Bad
Faith." West Africa, no. 3278, 1980, pp. 876-877.
The author, in an article reprinted from the Daily
Times of Nigeria, reflects on the wider implications
for journalism of the Vera Ifudu case. The article is
an attempt to throw more light on the circumstances
surrounding the dismissal of Vera Ifudu, the Nigerian
television Senate correspondent. There have been
instances where journalists were less justifiably
dismissed from their jobs. The dismissal of Vera Ifudu
was a glaring example of bad faith, if ever there was
any.

293. MACKAY, Ian K. Broadcasting in Nigeria. Ibadan:
University of Ibadan Press, 1964.
The only book length study of a single Black African
broadcasting system. Very authoritative book on
Nigerian broadcasting - and perhaps, the standard text
book on the subject.

294. MACKAY, Ian K. "Concepts of Nigerian
Broadcasting." E.B.U. Review, no. 78b, March 1963, pp.
15-20.
Describes the origin, pattern and trend of Nigerian
broadcasting as well as constitutional considerations
and regional government broadcasting.

295. MACKENZIE, W.J.M., & Kenneth Robinson. Five
Elections in Africa. New York: Oxford University
Press, 1960.
A description of the roles played by newspapers and
radio in pre-independence elections in Sierra Leone,
Kenya and Nigeria. The roles of these media of

communication in Eastern and Western regions of Nigeria are particularly discussed.

296. MACKINTOSH, John P. Nigerian Government and Politics: Prelude to the Revolution. Evanston, Illinois: Northwestern University Press, 1966.
Author examines the constitutional development of Nigeria, and particularly gives an account of the roots and development of the Newspaper Act of 1964, a press law that has remained unpopular in journalistic circles in Nigeria.

297. MADUKA, Vincent & Rufai Yahaya, "Television Development - Setting up a Modest Television Station," Combroad, no. 46, 1980, pp. 20-22.
A proposal for setting up a modest -- though not necessarily cheap -- color television station in a developing country such as Nigeria. The project is analyzed in the context of: a) broadcasting policy b) equipment selection and building, and c) personnel and manpower. The main conclusion is that given the size of the African village or community which is relatively small, the Nigerian television experience in community viewing supports the modest television concept.

298. MAPADERUN, Femi. "Routine Harassment or Detention of Journalists," IPI Report, vol. 24, nos. 4-5, 1975, p. 19.
Author outlines Nigeria's qualified press freedom. The main conclusion is that there is still at least one freedom left for journalists in Nigeria which makes them the envy of most other African states: They have the freedom to file court actions against any government officials who confront them physically.

299. MATHIAS, Hilletework. "Partisan Press and National Development in Nigeria: A Case Study." M.A. thesis, The American University, 1977.
The role of the Nigerian press as it treated a major issue - the national census - in the early 1960's, is studied to help assess the impact of the press on national development. The results show that the national dailies were biased in their editorial coverage of the census issue, thus making themselves a negative force in the development process.

300. MAY, Clifford D. "Nigeria: Who Won the Battle?" IPI Report, vol. 33, no. 6, 1984, p. 6.
This article contains a description of some of the provisions of Decree No. 4 of 1984 also known as "Public Officers (Protection Against False Accusation) Decree. The reactions of some Nigerian journalists to

the press law are also described. Instances of harassment of journalists by the military government are provided along with accounts of national and international protests to the Buhari government to repeal the obnoxious press law.

301. MEGWA, Eronini R. "Media Control and Professionalization: A Case Study of the Perception of News Policies by Editors and Reporters at Two Nigerian Television Stations." M.S. thesis, Iowa State University, 1982.
Does the government control what is broadcast to Nigerian listeners? Are editors and reporters autonomous in professional decision-making? This study concludes that Nigerian journalists employed in two government-owned broadcast stations have considerable autonomy in their professional decisions. However, because government exclusively owns the electronic media in the country, it indirectly controls some of the broadcast contents, especially on political issues.

302. MERRILL, John C. "Inclination of Nations to Control Press and Attitudes on Professionalization." Journalism Quarterly, Vol. 65, no. 4, 1988, pp. 839-844.
This study is an attempt to investigate the inclination to control the press by governments of fifty-eight countries, including Nigeria. In developing a Control Inclination Index (CII) for each country, the author uses six factors said to be important indicators of a propensity to control the press in rank ordering the potential of national governments to control the press through professionalization. Each of the six factors -- I) in-country licensing, 2) international licensing, 3) identification cards or accreditation, 4) university education, 5) in-country codes of ethics, and 6) international codes of ethics -- was given a score on a scale of zero to four, reflecting the strength of attitudes of that factor (e.g., very much in favor = 4 and very much against = 0). Nigeria scored 18 points on the CII scale, indicating that officials in the country were just in favor of press control through professionalization. Countries that had the same score with Nigeria on the CII scale are Poland, Portugal, Bangladesh, Indonesia and South Korea.

303. MGBEJUME, Oyero. Film in Nigeria: Development, Problems and Promise. Ph.D dissertation, The University of Texas at Austin, 1978.
This study looks at the problems and historical development of the motion picture industry in Nigeria from 1903, the first time films were shown publicly in

the country, through 1947 when the Nigerian government
established an indigenous film unit to early 1978.
Five major factors are identified as responsible for
the lack of growth in the industry: constraints posed
by colonialism, bureaucracy, lack of funds, absence of
trained Nigerian film makers and lack of recognition of
the importance of film on the part of Nigerians and
their leaders.

304. MGBEMENA, Nwabu N. Nigerian Journalists: A Study
of Their Demographic Characteristics and Professional
Orientation. Ph. D dissertation, University of Texas,
1980.
A profile of Nigerian journalists as seen through a
case study of eighty-three journalists drawn from eight
of the country's nineteen states. The study shows
that: 1) Nigerian journalism is dominated by
professionals from the nine southern states; 2) men
outnumber women in Nigerian journalism by a ratio of
9:1; 3) the journalists who work for the urban oriented
media are mostly urban bred scions of middle to high
income earners.

305. MILTON, Edward C. A Survey of the Technical
Development of the Nigerian Broadcasting Corporation.
Lagos: NBC 1955.
Examines the history and technical development of the
Nigerian Broadcasting Corporation -- NBC.

306. MINTAH, Conrad. "Television Program Co-
Production in Africa," Combroad, no. 48, 1980, pp. 18-
23.
Author makes a proposal for television program co-
production and exchange among African countries. The
example of such co-operation between Nordic television
station and Nigerian television during the 1977
festival of the arts and culture, FESTAC, is
highlighted. Efforts in the same direction by four
West African countries -- Sierra Leone, Liberia, Ghana
and Nigeria -- are mentioned along with some of the
problems of such cooperation.

307. MOMOH, Eddie, & Ad'Obe Obe. "The Dikko Affair:
The Kidnapping and After," West Africa, no. 3491 (July
16,1984), pp. 1432-1434.
How did the British and Nigerian press report the Umaro
Dikko attempted abduction from Britain in the summer of
1984? The British newspapers, including the Daily
Mirror, Daily Express, Daily Telegraph, The Times and
The Sun, endorsed the British government accusation
that the Buhari government had complicity in the
abortive abduction scheme. Conversely, the Nigerian

press, for example, the <u>Sunday Times</u> and <u>Sunday Concord</u> took sides with the Nigerian government in the diplomatic row between Britain and Nigeria.

308. MOMOH, Tony. "Various Press Laws 1903-1984." Paper presented at a symposium marking the 30th anniversary celebration of the Nigerian Union of Journalists at the National Theatre, Igamu, Lagos, May 1985.
An impressive attempt to examine the development and provisions of some of the colonial laws utilized by Britain to stifle freedom of expression in Nigeria.

309. MOMOH, Tony. "Nigeria: The Press and Nation-Building," <u>Africa Report</u>, March-April, 1987, pp. 54-57.
Nigeria's Federal Minister for Information and Culture examines the role of the nation's press in furthering national unity and development. The press has had an impact on the struggle toward decolonization, and has contributed substantially to the detection of graft and political corruption. The press has also played a crusading role on key issues in the public interest, and has been foremost in initiating and supporting community service.

310. MOSES, Sibyl E. "Nigerian Government Posters: Visual Records of People and Progress," <u>Government Publications Review</u>, vol. 7A, no. 3, 1980, pp. 221-227.
This article discusses and categorizes Nigerian government posters, and emphasizes their value for Nigerian libraries as examples of visual government publications.

311. MURPHY, Lloyd E. "Nationalism and the press in British West Africa," M.A. thesis, University of Wisconsin, 1967.
This study traces the development of the press in the former colonial British West African countries of Ghana, Nigeria, Sierra Leone and the Gambia. It also examines the role of the press in nationalism and the struggle for independence. It concludes that the press in Nigeria (as in these countries) was used as a more dynamic and revolutionary means than envisaged in the generally accepted "four theories of the press," thus possibly a new "theory" is evident. A list of Nigerian newspapers is provided in the appendix.

312. MYTTON, Graham. <u>Mass Communication in Africa</u>. London: Edward Arnold Publishers Ltd., 1983.
An overview of the development of mass communications in Africa. Author presents some useful information on

aspects of Nigerian press including government-press relations, journalistic practice and the involvement of the press in politics particularly between 1978 and 1981.

313. NAM, Sam & Inhwan Oh, "Press Freedom: Function of Subsystem Autonomy, Antithesis of Development," Journalism Quarterly, vol. 50, no. 4, 1973, pp. 744-750.
An attempt to explain the relationship between the developmental efforts of the governments and curtailment of press freedom in developing countries. Nigeria is mentioned in the study which shows relationships between press freedom and indirect measures of subsystem autonomy. The study also shows incompatibility between freedom and developmental efforts.

314. NDOLO, Ikechukwu S. Radio Broadcasting and the Language Problems of Socio-Political Integration in Nigeria. Ph. D. dissertation, Howard University, 1987. An examination of the role of radio broadcasting and the language problems of national integration in Nigeria. The study formulates an indigenous mass communication model for the achievement of socio-political integration of the multi-linguistic groups in the country. The model purposes that the Federal Government can achieve integration by restructuring the present radio broadcasting system, establishing one that uses the Nigerian Pidgin language (the language of widest communication) to broadcast uniformly structured national messages to all the ethnic groups simultaneously.

315. Newspapers in Microform: Foreign Countries 1948-1983. Washington, D.C.: Library of Congress, 1984. This publication is an accumulation of newspapers in microform from countries outside the United States. Compiled by the U.S. Library of Congress, it lists several Nigerian newspapers under the names of the cities in which the papers were published in the past or are still being published. The dates of the issues held in microform are given, and the names and addresses of libraries where the newspapers can be found are also provided.

316. Nigerian Broadcasting Corporation. NBC: Ten Years of Service. Lagos: NBC, 1967.
A publication of the Nigerian Broadcasting Corporation, describing the corporation's operation and service.

317. Nigerian Broadcasting Corporation, "Ten Years of
Service: A Story of Expansion." <u>Asian Broadcasting
Union Newsletter</u>, Vol. 46, no. 15, 1969.
A reflection on ten years of service by the Nigerian
Broadcasting Corporation (NBC). What the role of
Nigerian broadcasting should be is also mentioned.

318. <u>Nigerian Periodicals and Newspapers, 1950-1955</u>.
Ibadan: University College Library, n.d.
Provides a list of Nigerian periodicals and newspapers
received from April 1950 to June 1955 under the
publications ordinance, 1950.

319. <u>Nigeria Year Book</u>. Lagos: Times Press Limited,
1974.
A reference book that provides information about
Nigeria's socio-economic and political institutions,
including the press. This reference book which is up-
dated from time to time provides information on the
history of the press, names of editors and addresses of
printers of daily and weekly newspapers. Information
on periodicals and magazines is provided.

320. NIXON, Raymond B. "Freedom in the World's Press:
A Fresh Appraisal With New Data," <u>Journalism Quarterly</u>,
vol. 42, no. 1, 1965, pp. 3-14.
A follow-up of a 1960 study to assess freedom of
national press systems. A nine-point scale is used to
measure press freedom in one hundred, seventeen
countries, including Nigeria, which is ranked fairly
positively on the scale. Information on daily
circulation, number of radio, and television sets and
cinema theatre seats per one hundred people is provided
on the Nigerian press.

321. NIXON, Raymond B., & Tae Youl Hahn,
"Concentration of Press Ownership: A Comparison of 32
Countries," <u>Journalism Quarterly</u>, vol. 48, no. 1, 1971,
pp. 5-16.
A cross-national study of newspaper ownership in
thirty-two countries, including Nigeria. Using a
concentration Index, the study concludes that among
Third World countries, the press in Africa,
particularly Nigeria, Kenya and Zimbabwe, is controlled
to the highest degree by a few firms. Ninety-four
percent of the total daily circulation of newspapers in
Nigeria is controlled by four largest ownership units,
and 100% by eight largest ownership units.

322. NORD, Bruce A. "Press Freedom and Political
Structure," <u>Journalism Quarterly</u>, vol. 43, no. 3, 1966,
pp. 531-534.

An Annotated Bibliography

A comparison of the functioning of <u>Daily Graphic</u> of
Accra, Ghana and <u>Daily Times</u> of Lagos, Nigeria.
Differences in performance of both newspapers is
established through a quantitative picture of press
freedom -- the extent to which the papers criticize the
on-going political process -- drawn out of content
analysis. The <u>Daily Times</u> is more active and more
critical of the two papers. The <u>Times</u> is also bolder
in criticizing and naming government officials in its
editorials.

323. NORDENSTRENG, Kaarle and Tapio Varis. <u>Television
Traffic: A One-Way Street?</u> Reports and papers on Mass
Communication no. 70, Paris: Unesco, 1974.
Discusses U.S. dominance of the trade in syndicated
programs. The countries whose programs are inventoried
include Nigeria.

324. NWABUEZE, B.O. <u>Constitutional Law of the
Republic of Nigeria</u>. London: Butterworths, 1964.
Author examines the constitutional law of the Federal
Republic of Nigeria with special mention on press law.

325. NWANKWO, Nwafo R. <u>A Perspective on Communication
and the Development Press: Family Communication
Patterns and Role-Taking in an Urban Sub-Culture</u>. Ph.D
dissertation, university of Wisconsin, 1970.
This study looks at the relation of communication
process during socialization in the family to
adolescent's symbolic role-taking inside and outside
the family. It shows that an orientation to task or
achievement and high congruency in secondary relations
are suggested as having implications for communicative
modernity or a preference for obtaining information
from diverse sources.

326. NWAOZUZU, Hilary A. <u>Emeka Ojukwu's Rhetoric of
Secessionism and Yakubu Gowon's Anti-Secessionist
Rhetoric: A Critical and Historic Analysis</u>. Ph.D
dissertation, State University of New york at Buffalo,
1985.
An analysis of Emeka Odumegwu Ojukwu's agitational
rhetoric of secession and Yakubu Gowon's anti-
secessionist rhetoric as set forth in their selected
addresses and speeches during the Nigerian Civil War
(1967-1970). The main conclusion is that the
strategies identified in their speeches can also be
applied in the analysis of the contemporary rhetoric of
protest in such areas as politics and human relations.

327. NWOSU, Ikechukwu E. "Mass Media Discipline and
Control in Contemporary Nigeria: A Contextual Critical
Analysis," Gazette, vol. 39, no. 1, 1987, pp. 17-29.
A critical analysis of two aspects of mass
communication, disciplinary and control mechanisms in
Nigerian press: professional training, codes of ethics,
press council, press ombudsmanship and press laws. The
main conclusion is that presently, there are many
internal disciplinary and control mechanisms to ensure
a virile, responsible and efficient media system, and
more than enough laws and government actions to ensure
discipline and control from outside the media. But the
lack of internal enforcement mechanisms to ensure
discipline in the media sub-system has created room for
the seemingly excessive government meddlesomeness in
the form of laws and similar acts.

328. NWUNELI, Onuorah. "Broadcasting Regulation and
the Politicians of the First Nigerian Republic." Pan-
African Journal, vol. 6, no. 1, 1973. pp. 57-65.
Examines the role of the politicians of the first
Nigerian Republic in the regulation of the broadcasting
industry in Nigeria.

329. NWUNELI, Onuora E. "Socio-economic Status and
Mass Media Use in a Developing African Nation," Media
Asia, vol. 6, no. 2, 1979, pp. 76-78.
An examination of the relationships between socio-
economic status and mass media exposure habits among
residents in Lagos. Analysis of the data obtained in
the study shows that income and education are good
predictors of mass media exposure. But cinema
attendance is not related to either education or
income.

330. NWUNELI, Onuora E. Socio-Economic Status, Socio-
Economic Expectation and Mass Media Exposure in Lagos,
Nigeria. Ph.D dissertation, University of Wisconsin-
Madison, 1976.
This study investigates the relationships between the
socio-economic status of Lagos residents and their mass
media exposure habits. It also explores whether socio-
economic expectations of Lagosians could be a
determinant of their mass media use. The study
concludes that access and exposure to the media of mass
communication are associated with income and education.

331. NWUNELI, Onuora E., & Effiong Udoh,
"International News Coverage in Nigerian Newspapers,"
Gazette, vol. 29, no. 1/2, 1982, pp. 31-40.
What kinds of foreign news stories are published in
Nigerian newspapers and what parts of the world get

more coverage than others? These are the main research questions addressed. The study covers four one-year period (from December 1, 1978 to November 30, 1979), using the Daily Times, New Nigerian, Nigerian Chronicle, Daily Sketch and Punch newspapers. Results show that most of the foreign news in Nigerian newspapers is about Africa, and that the Nigerian press is heavily dependent on transnational wire news services for the coverage of world events, including events in Africa. More stories about the developing nations are published than about the Western or Eastern block countries.

332. OBIKA, D. D. "The Work of UNESCO and Other International Agencies to Improve the Standard of Journalism in Africa, South of Sahara." M.A. thesis, University of Missouri, 1969.
A discussion of the history of the involvement of UNESCO and other international agencies in the development of journalism in Africa, south of the Sahara. The objectives of these agencies and the reactions of African leaders toward them are also discussed. Nigeria is one of the countries covered in the study.

333. OBOTETTE, Bassey E. Mass Communication for National Development in Nigeria: Analysis of Content and Structure. Ph.D dissertation, Howard university, 1984.
To what degree has the Nigerian press participated in the process of national integration? This study concludes that the media are parochial in content and sectional in outlook, implying that the process of national integration through the media is yet to begin. Author argues that the Eurocentric concepts of development and the paradigms often associated with development communication are no more than a set of values drawn from the universal slogans of "free enterprise," and that these concepts and paradigms can neither measure the performance, nor prescribe the proper roles of the press in a developing nation like Nigeria.

334. OGAN, Christine L., & C. Swift. "Is the News About Development All Good?" Paper presented at the AEJMC Conference, Athens, Ohio, 1982.
An examination of the amount and nature of development news in important daily newspapers of Third World countries, including the New Nigerian of Nigeria. The study concludes that about half of the development news items in these newspapers, including the New Nigerian, are positive in tone and only about one-fourth of the

news in these newspapers contains information from critical sources.

335. OGAN, Christine L, Jo Ellen Fair & Hemant Shah, "A Little Good News: Development News in Third World Newspapers," In Communication Yearbook 8 (pp. 628-644). Beverly Hills, California: Sage Publications, Inc., 1984.
This study, a follow up of an earlier study by Christine Ogan and C. Swift, examines the nature and quantity of development news in selected third World newspapers. The Daily Times and New Nigerian of Nigeria are among the most important Third World newspapers used in this study which does not show much change or progress in the overall coverage of development news between the period of this study, 1984 and the period of previous study by Ogan and Swift, 1982.

336. OGAN, Christine L., & Jo Ellen Fair, "A Little Good News": The Treatment of Development News in Selected Third World Newspapers," Gazzette, vol. 33, no. 3, 1984, pp. 173-191.
Examines the treatment of "development news" in nine Third World newspapers. Among the newspapers selected from the University of Indiana library for the study are two influential Nigerian newspapers, Daily Times and New Nigerian.

337. OGBONDAH, Chris W. "Nigerian Journalism: A Bibliographical Essay," Gazette, vol. 36, no. 3, 1985, pp. 175-191.
A bibliographical essay using some of the major works published on Nigerian press under the following headings: freedom and censorship, history and politics. Author attempts to point out the weaknesses in some of these works, and also makes an effort to correct some erroneous statements in them so that future users of the works may not make the same mistakes made in them. How each work is similar or distinguishable from others is also pointed out. The author argues for the need for a work of annotated bibliography on Nigerian press.

338. OGBONDAH, Chris W. Nigeria's Decree no. 4: A Sword Against the Pen. Ph.D dissertation, Southern Illinois University at Carbondale, 1986.
A study of the most dreaded and repressive press law, Decree no. 4 of 1984 also known as "Public Officers (Protection Against False Accusation) Decree. The study examines the provisions of the law and its origins. The socio-political factors which helped shape the law as well as the law's impact on political

expression and press freedom are also examined. The
main conclusion is that the decree -- the sword of
damocles which hung directly over the Nigerian press --
 brought a chilling, even freezing effect on the press.
Ironically enough, however, suppression tended to lead
to more public expression against the decree.

339. OGBONDAH, Chris W. "Nigerian Press Under the
Generals." Paper presented at the Third World Studies
Conference, Omaha, Nebraska, October 16-17, 1986.
An examination of institutional measures adopted by
five military generals to control the Nigerian press.
The Generals include Aguiyi Ironsi, Yakubu Gowon,
Murtala mohammed, Olusegun Obasanjo and Muhammadu
Buhari. An attempt is made to compare press control
measures under these military leaders.

340. OGBONDAH, Chris W. "In the Wake of Military
Dictatorship: The Tribulation of Nigerian Press."
Paper Presented at the Southeast Regional Colloquium of
AEJMC, Blacksburg, Virginia, March 20, 1987.
An examination of government-press relations during the
military regime of Maj. Gen. Muhammadu Buhari. In
addition, the paper examines public reactions to the
military government's dictatorship with particular
reference to its relationship with the press.

341. OGBONDAH, Chris W. "Nigerian Journalism: An
Antithesis of Tradition." Paper presented at the
International Communication Association (ICA)
Conference in Montreal, Canada, May 1987.
This paper examines the institutional control measure
adopted by Maj. Gen. Muhammadu Buhari to tame the
normally vocal and vigorous Nigerian press from 1984 to
1985. The main conclusion is that journalistic freedom
under the Buhari regime was antithetical to the
tradition of Nigerian press freedom which dates beyond
the period of British colonial administration in
Nigeria.

342. OGBONDAH, Chris W. "Colonial Laws: Model for
Contemporary African Press Laws." Paper presented at
the 10th national Third World Studies Conference,
University of Nebraska, Omaha, October 1987.
The main conclusion of this paper is that the post-
independence African press laws may be just
reincarnations of the souls of colonial laws utilized
by France and Britain to control the African press,
especially the Nigerian press, during the colonial
period.

343. OGBONDAH, Chris W. "Alien Authoritarianism,
Indigenous Dictatorship and the Nigerian Press: A Study
of One Aspect of Nigerian Journalism History." Paper
presented at the 15th annual Midwest Journalism History
Conference, Columbus, Ohio, April 1988.
This paper identifies British colonial government and
military regimes in Nigeria as authoritarian in nature.
it examines how the indigenous population reacted to
press laws enacted by alien political authorities
(British colonial government) and the indigenous
(military) government in Nigeria. Two press laws, the
Newspaper Ordinance of 1903 and Decree No. 4 of 1984
are used as case studies.

344. OGBONDAH, Chris W. "Nigerian Press Under
Imperialists and Dictators, 1903-1985." Paper
presented at the annual meeting of the AEJMC at
Portland, Oregon, July 1988.
This is an extended version of the author's preceding
study. The study seeks to find out whether the
governed reacted more favorably toward press laws
enacted by indigenous military dictators than they did
toward those press laws enacted by British imperial
authorities. The study also seeks to find out the
variables that helped shape those laws as well as the
laws' objectives. The main conclusion is that the
governed vehemently opposed the introduction of press
laws which they did not participate in drafting -- at
least through elected representatives in government.
It did not matter to them who enacted such laws.

345. OGUNADE, Ademola. "Mass Media and National
Integration in Nigeria," In L. Erwin Atwood, Stuart J.
Bullion and Sharon M. Murphy (eds.), International
Perspectives on News (pp. 22-32). Carbondale, Illinois:
Southern Illinois University Press, 1982.
How the mass media could be used to achieve national
integration in Nigeria is the focus of this work. The
central argument of the work is that any understanding
of the utilization of the mass media to promote
national integration in a multiethnic nation such as
Nigeria, must be founded on an understanding of the
ideological orientation of that country's political
culture. The author also reflects the role of
newspapers in the Nigerian crisis.

346. OGUNADE, Ernest A. Freedom of the Press:
Government-Press Relationships in Nigeria, 1900-1966.
Ph.D dissertation, Southern Illinois University at
Carbondale, 1981.
The author examines the Nigerian government
relationship with the press in the context of freedom

of the press over a period of sixty-five years.   It
concludes that if the relationships between the press
and government have to improve, the press must become
autonomous; constitutional as well as legal guarantees
of press freedom must be made explicit and broadly
construed by the judiciary and a cadre of courageous,
professionally competent, and public spirited
journalists needs to emerge.

347.   OGUNSHEYE, Ayo.   "Education in Public Affairs by
Radio in Nigeria," Fundamental and Adult Education, no.
9, 1957, pp. 186-189.
This article deals with educational radio with special
focus on radio forum experiments.

348.   OGUNTAYO, E.O.   "A Nigerian View on the Design
and Manufacturing of Low-Cost Receivers," Combroad,
July-September, 1975, pp. 21-25.

349.   OGUNWALE, Titus, "Moves to Form Nigerian Press
Council May Follow New News Agency,"   IPI Report, vol.
25, no. 8, 1976, p. 5.
Reports the establishment of the Nigerian News Agency
which came by a Federal Military Government decree.
This report outlines the objectives of the new news
agency.   The author hopes that the setting up of the
agency could generate the right climate for examining
the issue of a press council.

350.   OGUNWALE, Titus.   "Punishment Powers `Are
Wrong'," IPI report, vol. 28, no. 2., 1979, pp. 11-12.
A description of the responsibility of the Nigerian
Press Council established by a Federal Military
Government decree.   Some of its flaws are pointed out,
and the public's reaction to the newly created council
are also described.   The author argues that with press
opposition of the council, it is unlikely that the
council will take off as planned by the military
government.

351.   OGUNWALE, Titus.   "A Rough Time For Nigeria's
Newsmen," IPI Reports, vol. 30, no. 6, 1981, pp. 14-
15.
Reviews the forced cover-price rises of newspapers and
the spate of arrests and harassments of journalists
from 1979 to 1981.   Many a journalist have been
downgraded, intimidated, blackmailed or removed from
offices.   A radio station in Kano was burnt down and
there were occasions when tapes were seized from
broadcasting studios.   In the context of the country's
new constitution therefore, an editor enjoyed no

freedom other than the freedom enjoyed by an ordinary
citizen.

352. OGUNWALE, Titus. "Nigeria Spreads Out," IPI
Report, vol. 29, no. 8, 1981, p. 14.
A report on the expansion of newspaper industry in
Nigeria. In 1960 when Nigeria became independent there
were about five dailies and ten weekly papers in the
country. The number of dailies had risen to thirteen
since the military took over power in 1966. The
biggest threat to the existence of newspapers in
Nigeria is perhaps the cut-back in the world supply of
newsprint and the increasingly prohibitive cost of
production. Transportation and distribution of
newspapers is also a problem.

353. OGUNWALE, Titus. "President Slams Nigerian Press
Bill," IPI Report, vol. 31, no. 10, 1982.
Describes the provision of Section 119 of a press
censorship bill signed into law in 1982 by President
Shehu Shagari as part of the 1982 Electoral Bill
designed to regulate the electoral processes in the
1983 general elections. This article also contains the
Nigerian Press Organization's reaction to the bill.
The organization is a central body made up of the
Newspaper Proprietors' Association of Nigeria (NPAN),
Nigerian Guild of Editors (NGE) and Nigerian Union of
Journalists (NUJ).

354. OGUNWALE, Titus. "Nigerian Media Calls For
Police Protection." IPI Report, vol. 32, no. 5, p. 7,
1983.
Describes some of the acts of sabotage, arson and
vandalism in Nigeria's media industry, and the actions
taken by the NPAN and the Nigerian Guild of Editors to
check further occurrences.

355. OGUNWALE, Titus. "State Lashes `Prostitute'
Press," IPI Report, vol. 32, no. 5, 1983, p. 7.
A report of the criticism of Nigerian press by two well
known national figures -- Dr. Nnamdi Azikiwe, a veteran
journalist with thirty-eight years experience and first
ceremonial president of Nigeria, and Lateef Jakande,
former chairman of International Press Institute, and
governor of Lagos State. The two veteran journalists
and political leaders accused Nigerian journalists of
prostituting the profession by disseminating extremely
partisan propaganda. The report contains similar
criticism of the press by another state governor.

356. OGUNWALE, Titus. "Prisoners," IPI Report, vol.
33, no. 12, 1984, p. 4.

An Annotated Bibliography

A report of a world-wide appeal by the Executive Board of the International Press Institute for the release of Lateef Jakande, former IPI Chairman who was relieved of his duty as editor of Nigerian Tribune to serve as governor of Lagos state. The report also contains an account of a Lagos High Court ruling that awarded about $15,375 to a Nigerian journalist for wrongful arrest and detention by the police.

357. OGUNWALE, Titus. "No News is Bad News," IPI Report, vol. 34, no. 7, 1984, p. 7.
A look at the consequences of the New Street and Illegal Markets (Prohibition) Amendment law introduced during the Buhari regime, on newspaper sales and readership. The law was short-lived.

358. OGUNWALE, Titus. "Nigeria Jails Radio Chief in Bribe Case," IPI Report, vol. 34, no. 1, 1985, p. 4.
An account of the jailing of three chief executives of Kano State Radio Corporation in northern Nigeria. The executives were sentenced to a total of sixty-six years after being found guilty of demanding and receiving about $35,000 from a communication equipment supply firm. A distinction is made between the trial of the three media executives and two editors of the Guardian also jailed by the same military government.

359. OGUNWALE, Titus. "Court Resolves NUJ Leadership Dispute," IPI Report, vol. 34, no. 3, 1985, p. 16.
A report of a Lagos High Court ruling, resolving a long-drawn out leadership tussle in the Nigerian Union of Journalists (NUJ). An attempt to examine some of the implications of the court decision is made.

360. OGUNWALE, Titus. "Nigeria: Learning the Lessons," IPI Report, vol. 34, no. 5, 1985, p. 4.
An examination of some of the implications of the imprisonment and release of two Guardian journalists jailed under Decree no. 4 of 1984. The author believes that the release of the journalists heralded the dawn of an ethical revolution in Nigerian journalism, and concludes that Nigerian journalists must be prepared to make greater sacrifice than ever before or in default, sell out to the visibly transient might of the clique.

361. OGUNWALE, Titus. "Military Tightens Broadcast Network," IPI Report, vol. 33, no. 5, 1985, p. 14.
A report of Maj. Gen. Muhammadu Buhari government's plan to restructure and centralize Nigeria's elaborate broadcasting industry. The federal government's three major objectives for the action are given. The

economic and social implications for the centralization exercise are analyzed.

362. OGUNWALE, Titus. "Opening the Gates of Oppression," IPI Report, vol. 34, no. 10, 1985, p. 5. An account of the abrogation of Decree no. 4 of 1984 as well as some of the effects of the law on press freedom. The author seems to hold the view that the repeal of the hated press law is a good sign for freedom of expression in Nigeria.

363. OGUNWALE, Titus. "Nigeria Guarantees Free Speech," IPI Report, vol. 35, no. 4, 1986, p. 7. A reflection on Ibrahim Babangida's military government attitude toward the press. According to the author, the federal government has a more or less liberal policy toward the press, and is deeply committed to the patronage of multiple mass media ownership and expression.

364. OGUNWALE, Titus. "Nigeria's Recession Renews Old Rivalry," IPI Report, vol. 35, no. 7, 1986, p. 6. This article profiles the conflict between the Newspaper Proprietors Association of Nigeria (NPAN) and the Association of Advertising Practitioners of Nigeria (AAPN) over who should handle the business of advertising in the midst of worsening national economic problems.

365. OGUNWALE, Titus. "Nigeria Seeks a Workable Press Council," IPI Report, vol. 35, no. 9, 1986, pp. 12-13. The new government of president Ibrahim Babangida has invited journalists and academicians to help set the agenda for a new press council that could benefit everyone; but first they need to reach common accord. The views of scholars, journalists and the government on the new press council are presented.

366. OKEDIJI, F.O. "Mass Communication Media in Public Health Promotion in Nigeria: Problems and Prospects," Nigerian Opinion, vol. 2, no. 12, 1966, pp. 142-144. An analysis of the role of the mass media in public health promotion. The author believes that the role of the media in this respect has been minimal, and suggests ways of increasing the effectiveness of radio, television, newspapers and cinema as well as inter-personal communication in public health promotion. There is the need for the ministries of information, health and economic planning to cooperate in order to achieve a well rounded public health education of the masses.

367. OKIGBO, Charles. "The Brain Drain' and International Communication," In Robert N. Bostrom (Ed.), Communication Yearbook 7 (pp. 554-573). Beverly Hills, California: Sage Publications, Inc., 1983. This study provides some information on media use patterns, and tends to suggest that Nigerian students who return to the country after studying in the United States of America, attend more to Nigerian communication -- Nigerian newspapers, magazines and embassy publications -- while those who remain in the U.S. after studying attend more to American media.

368. OKIGBO, Charles. "Nigerian High School Students Evaluate Journalism Careers," Journalism Quarterly, vol. 61, no. 4, 1984, pp. 907-909. A pilot study undertaken to determine the attitudes of some Nigerian high school students towards choosing journalism as a career. The results of the study which was done, using a sample of secondary school students in Enugu suggest that more Nigerian women will be entering journalism career in the years ahead.

369. OKIGBO, C.C. "News Flow Imbalance: Quantifications of Nigerian Press Content," Gazette, vol. 36, no. 2, 1985, pp. 95-107. Five Nigerian newspapers -- National Concord, The Guardian, Daily Times, New Nigerian, and Statesman -- are used to determine the nature of foreign news coverage in Nigerian press. Nigerian newspapers devote a high percentage (68%) of their news space to local events and personalities, while international news is given about a third of the total news as a whole. The main conclusion is that the Third World account for about 88% of the total news content, while the rest of the world accounts for only 12%. The focus of Nigerian papers is therefore regional (Third World) and the emphasis is local (Nigeria) -- a strong evidence of both quantitative and qualitative bias in Nigerian press coverage of foreign news.

370. OKIGBO, Charles. "World News in Nigerian Newspapers," In Margaret L. Melaughlin (Ed.), Communication Yearbook 9 (pp. 261-274). Beverly Hills, California: Sage Publications, Inc., 1986. Is the Nigerian press guilty of biases in its foreign news coverage? The author says yes, it is. Based on analysis of data from five Nigerian newspapers -- The National Concord, Daily Times, New Nigerian, The Guardian and Nigerian Statesman -- this study concludes that the Nigerian press is guilty of the same biases for which Western journalists are being criticized.

371. OKIGBO, Charles. "Death and Funeral Ads in the
Nigerian Press," Journalism Quarterly, vol. 64, nos. 2
& 3, 1987, pp. 629-633.
This study attempts to determine the major content
characteristics of obituary ads in Nigerian newspapers
using the Daily Times and National Concord. The main
conclusion is that obituaries are dominant features of
the newspaper press such that they have become the most
noticeable identifying marks. Obituaries in the press
reflect the values of society and contain many
statements that suggest the prevailing beliefs and
attitudes of the people.

372. OKIGBO, Charles. "Nigerian Radio News and the
New Information Order." Gazette, Vol. 41, no. 3, 1988,
pp. 141-150.
This study set out to determine if there is evidence of
quantitative and/or qualitative imbalance against the
outside world in news coverage by Nigerian radio
corporation.
Using news broadcasts by the Federal Radio Corporation
of Nigeria (FRCN), Lagos and Anambra Broadcasting
Service (ABS), Radio One, Enugu, the study found that
not only are outside countries neglected
quantitatively, they are also unfairly reported
qualitatively in Nigerian radio news broadcasts. The
Study also found that Nigerian journalism as
exemplified by radio news coverage, does not provide
adequate coverage of the rural parts of the country,
and therefore guilty of quantitative and qualitative
biases, just as the media in the developed countries
are guilty of unfair coverage of the developing
countries.

373. OKONKWOR, Chude R. The Press and Nigerian
Nationalism, 1859-1960. Ph.D dissertation, University
of Minnesota, 1976.
The issue addressed in this study is the role of the
press in Nigerian nationalism in the period 1859, when
the first Nigerian newspaper was born and 1960, the
year Nigeria became an independent nation. One of the
principal hallmarks of the Nigerian press is the
remarkable role it played in developing, sustaining and
crystallizing Nigerian nationalism. The study also
shows that while the press mobilized the people, it
also influenced the British in the formulation of
colonial legislation, thereby hastening the handing
over of political power by Britain to Nigerians.

374. OKONKWOR, Chude R and Everette E. Dennis. "Final
Exams Nigerian Style: An Accreditation Alternative?"

An Annotated Bibliography

Journalism Educator, vol. 35, no. 3, 1980, pp. 15-17,
54.
To what extend should the end product of journalism
education -- the competency of students -- figure into
the evaluation or accreditation of a particular
program?   This is the main research question raised in
this study.   A casual comparison is made between the
professional school accreditation in the United States
and the practice of using external examiners to
evaluate the quality of journalism education or degree
programs in Nigerian universities.   Some of the
liabilities of the Nigerian practice and what
indigenous students think about it are mentioned.   The
authors tend to suggest that the use of external
examiners to assess the quality of journalism degree
and overall degree programs in Nigerian universities
might be the alternative to the professional school
accreditation in the United States.

375.   OKONKWOR, Chude R.   "Nigeria's Sedition Laws -
Their Effect on Free Speech,"   *Journalism Quarterly*,
vol 62, no. 1, 1983, pp. 54-60.
In this article, the author traces the origins of
suppression of speech and other forms of expression in
Nigeria.   The British colonial administrators enacted
laws that kept the press from inciting a gullible
populace to hatred, disloyalty or violence against the
government.   The Federal Republic of Nigeria inherited
and utilized these laws at the dawn of independence.
These laws still have some effects on free speech in
Nigeria.

376.   OKONKWOR Chude R.   "The Press and the Formation
of Pre-Independence Political Parties in Nigeria,"
Nigeria Magazine, no. 137, 1981, pp. 66-72.
The organizational aspects of Nigerian nationalism
which matured in the form of political parties owed
much to the mobilization and integration fostered by
Nigerian newspaperman from early 1900's to the eve of
independence in 1960.   On the other hand, these parties
also helped to keep alive those newspapers, making the
overall picture that of the right hand washing the left
hand and the left washing the right.

377.   OKWUDISHU, Chris O.   "An Analysis of the Present
State of Television Broadcasting in the Federal
Republic of Nigeria With Particular Emphasis on Some of
the Problems that the Industry Faces in its Efforts to
Achieve its Goals."   M.A. thesis, Southern Illinois
University at Carbondale, 1980.
An examination of the state of television broadcasting
with particular emphasis on some of the many problems

it faces in its efforts to achieve the goals set out for industry. Some problems of television broadcasting are highlighted. The author believes that some objectives have been achieved but the Nigerian Television Authority will achieve greater heights if it takes stock of what has been achieved so far, what problems beset the industry and how these problems can be solved.

378. OLORUNSOLA, Victor A. Soldiers and Power: The Development Performance of the Nigerian Military Regime. California: Hover Institute, Stanford University, 1977.
The author uses primary source in a section of this book to describe the performance of the press under military rule. The author tends to contend that the press was bold enough to criticize the manner the government spent public funds, neglecting the welfare of the masses.

379. OLOWU, Terry A. "A Determination of the Readability of Nigerian Institute For Oil Palm Research (NIFOR) Advisory Sheets." M.A. thesis, University of Wisconsin, 1981.
A study designed to test the effectiveness of the advisory sheets -- publications put out by the Nigerian Institute for Oil Palm Research (NIFOR) -- in getting agricultural information across to both extension agents and local farmers. Results of the study show that NIFOR advisory sheets are somewhat difficult for the intended audience to understand: They are written in a language above the comprehension of the audience. When re-written with effective writing principles, they are easier read and understood.

380. OLUSOLA, Segun. "Firm Government Regulations Needed For Media in Nigeria," Combroad, no. 52, 1981, pp. 20-23.
This article examines the issue of ownership and control of television industry in Nigeria. The main point raised is that the private sector may not be allowed to participate in television ownership until such a time when through government control, national objectives have been set, operating regulations formulated and standards in quality of materials promulgated by the national and state governments.

381. OMU, Fred. "The Iwe Irohin," Journal of the Historical Society of Nigeria, vol.4, No. 1, 1967.
A discussion on the first Nigerian newspaper of which there is a record, the Iwe Irohin. The author describes the factors that made the paper's establishment

possible, and also explains the events that led to its abrupt end in October 1867.

382. OMU, Fred. "The Nigerian Press and the Great War," Nigerian Magazine, no. 96, 1968, pp. 44-49. This article examines the role of the Nigerian press during World War I. The press did not only wage a war of words against the Germans from 1914 to 1918, but it also gave considerable attention to campaigns to promote operations in various theatres of the war overseas. Four weekly owner-edited newspapers, the Record, the Lagos Standard, the Times of Nigeria and the Nigerian Pioneer, comprised the Nigerian press when the war broke out. The author also discusses the disagreement between Governor Frederick Lugard and James Bright-Davis, editor of the Times of Nigeria over the right of the press to criticize the handling of the war effort.

383. OMU, Fred. "The Dilema of Press Freedom in Colonial Africa: The West African Example," Journal of African History, vol. 9, no. 2, 1968, pp. 279-298. An authentic examination of press freedom in West African countries during the colonial period. Valuable information on Nigerian press freedom, especially the relationship between editors and colonial governors, is provided.

384. OMU, Fred. I.A. Press and Politics in Nigeria 1880-1937. Atlantic Highlands, New jersey: Humanities Press, 1978. An often-referenced source, this book is the most complete work on Nigerian press history up to 1937. it describes the role of the newspaper press and pioneer journalists in the nationalist movement for independence. It also provides a detailed table showing names of early newspapers, their editors, printers, addresses and the years during which they were published.

385. ONU, P.E. "The Use and Misuse of Scarce Newsprint: Mortuary Advertisements Compete For Space in African Daily Newspapers," Gazette, vol. 27, no. 2, 1981, pp. 105-121. The author examines the proportional distribution of space to various content categories in two African newspapers, the Ghanaian Times and the Daily Times of Nigeria. The prominence of mortuary advertisements coupled with their distinctive formats, suggests that they are a genre distinct from consumer goods and services advertisements.

386.   ONWUMERE, Emmanuel C.   "The Role of Television in
the Development of Nigeria."   M.A. thesis, North Texas
State University, 1983.
An attempt to show how television has affected the
politics, education, economy and religions in Nigeria.
A brief history of the broadcasting industry is given.
Author contends that television has raised the
consciousness and interests of Nigerians in political
activities, just as it has been an informative,
moderating and conciliatory influence on the divisive
elements in the country.

387.   ONYEDIKE, Emmanuel U.   "Origin and Development of
Press Laws in Nigeria."   M.A. thesis, University of
Iowa, 1979.
What actions did the government take to restrain the
press?   What factors prompted restraints on the press?
These are some of the questions addressed in this
study.   The results of government-press confrontations
are also discussed.   The main conclusion is that the
introduction of press laws was in response to newspaper
opposition and attacks on the government.

388.   ONYEDIKE, Emmanuel U.   "Government-Press
Relations in Nigeria: Effects of the Press Laws,"
Gazette, vol. 34, no. 2, 1984, pp. 91-102.
Author examines the origin, circumstances and
development of press laws in Nigeria, highlighting the
legal and political constraints of the laws on
journalistic practice.   Although intimidating, these
laws in the past did not deter some journalists'
efforts to safeguard freedom of expression.   Author
concludes that government-press relations will remain
sour as long as stringent, restrictive and obnoxious
press laws remain in the statute books.

389.   ONYEDIKE, Emmanuel U.   Journalism Education and
Newspaper Work in Nigeria. Ph.D dissertation, The
University of Iowa, 1985.
An assessment of the extent to which Nigerian newspaper
editors regard formal journalism education as a
necessary preparation for individuals involved in
newspaper work in Nigeria.   According to the study,
Nigerian editors hold the view that degree-holding
journalists are more knowledgeable or better skilled
than non-degree holding journalists in such areas as
knowledge of structure and processes of Nigeria,
ability to use tools of expression properly, and
possession of initiative, while non-degree-holding
journalists are more knowledgeable or better skilled
than degree-holding journalists in such areas as press
laws, newspaper layout and design and display of

dependability. Recommendations are made on how to
improve formal journalism education and practice.

390. ONYEDIKE, Emmanuel U. "The Nigerian Journalist's
Dilemma." Paper presented at the AEJMC conference in
Baton Rouge, Louisiana, 1985.
This paper highlights the ethical problems posed by the
employer-employee relationship in Nigerian journalism.
It also discusses media-ownership patterns and some
press legislations, and attempts to show how they
affect the performance of journalistic duties.

391. ONYEDIKE, Emmanuel U. "Journalism Education and
Newspaper Work in Nigeria." Paper presented at the
AEJMC at San Antonio, Texas, August 1987.
How can formal journalism education be improved in
Nigeria? To answer this question, the author compares
university degree with non-university degree holding
journalists on knowledge, competency and personal
quality attributes needed to work in newspapers. The
comparison indicates the strengths and weaknesses of
formal journalism curricula. Recommendations for
improving journalism education in Nigeria include the
introduction of internships for journalism students and
inclusion of practicing journalists and lawyers as part
of the teaching staff.

392. ONYEDIKE, Emmanuel U. "Revamping Nigerian
Journalism: The Roles of Government, Judiciary and
Journalists." Paper presented at the 10th National
Third World Studies Conference, University of Nebraska,
Omaha, October 1987.
Author contends that the press is capable of performing
creditably in spite of enormous legal, political and
economic obstacles. It requires the efforts of
government, journalists and the judiciary to revamp the
journalism profession in Nigeria. Six recommendations
-- at least two of them, provoking -- are made on how
to improve the profession.

393. ONYIA, A.N. "Mobile Units in Nigerian
Television," Combroad, no. 50, 1981, pp. 18-20.
A look at the beginning and operations of mobile
television units particularly used in the coverage of
outdoor events such as on-the-spot newsgathering,
airport interviews, regular coverage of soccer matches
and other national and international events. The
author tends to regret the decline of the use of these
mobile units despite enormous reduction in their cost
and increased efficiency.

394. ONYIA, A.N. "Engineering Problems in Television Broadcasting in Nigeria," Combroad, no. 60, 1983, pp. 30-32.
Director of engineering at Nigerian Television Authority describes the beginnings of television broadcasting in Nigeria. Technical and engineering problems in the process of that development are specially highlighted.

395. OPARA, Ralph. "Role of Radio as a Patron of Arts in Nigeria," Combroad, no. 65, 1984, pp. 17-19.
This article looks at some of the ways the Federal Radio Corporation of Nigeria -- formerly Nigerian Broadcasting Corporation -- has contributed to the nation's artistic development. Nigerian radio has supported the sponsorship of arts by bringing to the limelight, distinguished indigenous musicians, and by endorsing such cultural events as the Festival of Arts. The author deplores the declining role of radio in this respect.

396. OSOBA, Segun. "Country Reports: Nigeria," IPI Report, vol. 33, no. 8, 1984, p. 10.
A flash-on-the pan analysis of some of Nigeria's press laws with special focus on Decree no. 4 of 1984 -- the press law that sharply curbed press freedom during the twenty-month Buhari regime. An interesting distinction is made between this law and Decree no. 11 of 1976. Author contends that for publishers and editors in Nigeria, the newspaper industry is loaded with terrifying legal mines.

397. OSOBA, Segun. "Limitations of Censorship: Restraints on the Media," IPI Report, vol. 34, no. 4, 1985, p. 8.
An examination of the climate of press freedom and censorship in Nigeria. Author looks at legal and "extra-legal" constraints on the Nigerian press. The conclusion is that despite the constraints, the press will continue to resist every effort by governments to censor it, and there is a positive indication of success in that respect.

398. OTHMAN, Shehu. "Nigeria: On Decree no. 4," West Africa, no. 3550 (September 9, 1985), pp. 1845-1846.
In this article, the author reflects on Decree no. 4 of 1984 with special focus on the press law's immediate origin, its effect on journalistic freedom and reactions from a part of the press. Steps taken by Nigerian journalists to avoid the legal mine that was Decree no. 4, are also mentioned.

399. OREH, O.O. "The Beginnings of Self Censorship in Nigeria's Press and Mass Media," Gazette, vol. 22, no. 3, 1976, pp. 150-155.
Government takeover of Nigeria's formerly independent newspapers and mass media of communication from the 1960's to 1974, seemed to indicate the beginning of censorship in the press, and the end of freedom of speech among the citizens.

400. OTON, Esukema U. "Development of Journalism in Nigeria," Journalism Quarterly, vol. 35, no. 1, 1958, pp. 72-79.
All daily newspapers in Nigeria are published in English, and a few measure up to European and American standards. But technical difficulties and lack of trained personnel are serious handicaps. The article surveys the growth of Nigerian journalism from 1880 to 1958 and describes some leading newspapers. The author has done pioneer works on Nigerian journalism and Liberian press.

401. OTON, Esukema U. "The Training of Journalists in Nigeria," Journalism Quarterly, vol. 43, no. 1, 1966, pp. 107-109.
In this paper, the author identifies two major things about Nigerian journalism. For one, the mass media industry is rapidly expanding. For another, there is a shortage of trained journalists to mann the expanding industry. The paper points out the main areas in which such training had proceeded.

402. OUDES, Bruce. "The Other Nigerian War," Africa Report, vol. 15, no. 2, 1970, pp. 15-17.
There was too much of the wrong kind of news coverage of the Civil War as the foreign press took on the Federal Military Government of Nigeria in a storm of misunderstanding, distrust, and confusion. The author traces the influence of the press in Nigeria, particularly its role in publicizing the harsher aspects of the war. The author concludes that there are no more resourceful, thick-headed, and primitive guerrilla fighters in the world than correspondents.

403. OZIRI, Hilary M. The Evolution of Telecommunication in Nigeria: A Needs Analysis. Ph.D dissertation, State university of New York at Buffalo, 1984.
This study traces the evolution of telecommunication -- telephones, post and telex, television and radio -- and the print media from the colonial period of Nigerian history to early 1980's. Author also examines the role of the media in national development and modernization.

The main contention is that the mass media should be
used to impact upon national integration, education and
national economy such that the quality of life will be
improved for all Nigerians.

404. PARK, A.E. The Sources of Nigerian Law. Lagos:
African Universities Press, 1963.
Provides information on various laws governing the
Nigerian press, and attempts to trace the origins of
the press laws. The author contends that the roots of
Nigerian press laws are found in Britain. He argues
that Nigeria has enjoyed a tradition of press laws
since its early days as a British colony, and today's
press laws have British heritage.

405. PETT, Dennis W. Factors Affecting the
Institutionalization of the U.S.A.I.D/India University
Communications Media Project in Nigeria. Ph.D
dissertation, Indiana University, 1966.
This study is concerned with an analysis of factors
which affected the development and growth of
communications media facilities in Nigeria, following a
1959 Indiana university contract with the United States
International Cooperation Administration aimed at
assisting in the development of communication media
facilities in Nigeria. The study suggests several
guidelines for the development of communication media
projects not only in Nigeria but also in other
developing countries.

406. "Pin in a Bomb-Stack," Newswatch, November 10,
1986, pp. 15-22.
An in-depth discussion of the events and questions
surrounding the death of Newswatch editor-in-chief,
Dele Giwa, who was brutally murdered with a parcel bomb
on November 19, 1986.

407. POST, K.W. J. The Nigerian Federal Elections of
1959: Politics and Administration in a Developing
Political System. London: Oxford university Press,
1963.
A study of the federal elections of 1959, and the role
of the newspaper and other channels of communication
during the electioneering campaigns. Political
partisanship in the press is described.

408. PRATT, Cornelius. "Public Relations in the Third
World: The African Context," Public Relations
Journal, vol. 41, no. 2, 1985, pp. 11-12, 15-16.
Based on a field research conducted in West Africa, the
author looks at the concept of social responsibility
within the context of public relations practice in the

Third World. In Nigeria, public relations programs of
social, economic and political institutions are
designed to contribute toward national development.
Some of the objectives of the Nigerian Institute of
Public Relations are mentioned. The author also
provides some "ropes to know" and "ropes to skip" for
U.S. multinational corporations' public relations in
the Third World.

409. PRATT, Cornelius. "Communicating Population
Issues in Sub-Saharan Africa: A Development Policy For
Nigeria," Gazette, vol. 37, no. 4, 1986, pp. 169-189.
Author attempts to provide guidelines for formulating a
communication policy on limiting population growth in
sub-Saharan Africa, particularly Nigeria. The main
conclusion is that support services and social change
agencies should develop communication programs that
will attract nation-wide support by involving the
diverse social and cultural institutions in the
information-dissemination process in limiting family
size, increasing their receptivity to, and adoption of
family planning practices.

410. PRIDE, Cletis G. How Seven Commonwealth
Newspapers Reported Foreign Affairs, 1956-1968: A
Content Analysis. Ph.D dissertation, University of
North Carolina, 1969.
The purpose of this research is to analyze text devoted
to international affairs as it appeared in seven high
prestige English language newspapers of the
commonwealth. Among them was the West African Pilot of
Nigeria. The study shows among other things, that the
Pilot displayed strong regional interests, devoting a
substantial share of its total symbols to Africa. This
study points to yet another way of looking at the
journalism of Nigeria's once very most powerful
newspaper.

411. PRIDE, Cletis, "Content Analysis of Seven
Commonwealth Newspapers," Journalism Quarterly, vol.
49, no. 4, 1972, pp. 753-756.
An analysis of foreign affairs content in seven English
language newspapers of the British Commonwealth over a
thirteen-year period, 1956 through 1968. The West
African Pilot of Nigeria, the paper at the forefront of
the movement for nationalism during a part of the
period for the study, was among the seven newspapers
studied. The Nigerian newspaper's content seemed most
commonwealth-oriented, and although it showed
considerable interest in other African Commonwealth
members, the major source of symbols in the Pilot was
the United Kingdom.

412. <u>Publishing in Nigeria</u>. Benin City, Nigeria:
Ethiopa Publishing Corporation, 1972.
An anthology in which each individual article
represents an aspect of book publishing in Nigeria,
where for economic rather than political reasons, it is
under government control. Among the topics emphasized
are book development and publishing for children.

413. PURI, Shamlal. "London - Home of Africa's Top
Magazines," <u>IPI Report</u>, vol. 34, no. 7, 1985, p. 8.
Author attempts to explain the reasons for which London
has become the center of a boom in magazine publishing
for the African market. Nigerian magazines and their
publishers are prominently mentioned in the article.

414. PURISCH, Christine W. "Wole Soyinka: A Critical
Analysis of His Poetry." M.A. thesis, Duquesne
University, 1972.
A critical study of the poetry of professor Wole
Soyinka, one of Nigeria's top-flight writers, political
commentator and literature nobel prize winner. The
study focusses on Soyinka as an African writer and his
biographical background. Special analysis is made of
his major poem, <u>Idanre</u> and his use of dark and light
images. Author also dwells on Soyinka's political
expressions and imprisonments between 1965 and 1969.

415. RALPH, John. "A Study of News About Negroes in
the United States as Reported by Three Nigerian
Newspapers." M.A. thesis, Southern Illinois University
at Carbondale, 1966.
The extent to which several selected daily Nigerian
newspapers portrayed various aspects of the life of the
African-American in the United States, is the focus of
this study. Three papers --<u>Daily Times</u>, <u>Nigerian
Outlook</u> and <u>Daily Express</u> -- are studied. Negro
leadership, demonstrations, civic action and federal
government leadership were reported favorably while
unfavorable news coverage was given to state
government, police actions, treatments in the South and
North and portrayal of the Negro's position in the
United States.

416. ROBINSON, Deanna C. "Youth and Popular Music: A
Theoretical Rationale For an International Study,"
<u>Gazette</u>, vol. 37, nos. 1-2. 1986, pp. 34-49.
This work is a preliminary sketch of the theoretical
framework for an international study of youth and music
interaction. Conducted by the International
Communication and Youth Culture Consortium (ICYC), an
international research team made up of forty media
scholars in twenty-five countries, including Nigeria,

the study provides a flash-on-the pan picture of
Nigerian youth and music interaction. For example, the
study explains that Nigerian youth may have related to
the Beatles' music because they knew the Beatles were
from working-class families.

417. ROGER, Penn. "Broadcasting in Nigeria." M.A.
thesis, American University, Washington, D.C., 1960.
Examines the history, structure and development of
broadcasting industry in Nigeria.

418. ROSE, E.J.B. "Training is Most Urgent Need For
African Press," IPI Report, vol. 10, no. 9, 1962, pp.
1-3.
As Africa achieved independence in the 1960's, the
press was seen to pass more and more into the hands of
Africans. But inadequate training and political
hazards are problems facing the development of Africa's
press, in the view of the author, who visited ten
African countries, including Nigeria in the early
1960's. Nigeria is, however, seen as more advanced
than other African countries in terms of the
infrastructure for training journalists and in actual
practice of press freedom. Although there are certain
disquietening signs, the author believes that freedom
of the press would survive in Nigeria.

419. ROSE, E.J.B. "What Chance For the Press in West
Africa?" IPI Report, vol. 9, no. 5, 1960, pp. 6-7.
A review of the first-ever seminar attended by
journalists, from eight West African countries,
including Nigeria, on the prospects for the West
African press. The editors and journalists were
divided on the nature and philosophy of the press.
Right at the outset M. Doudou Gueye, the Senator for
Senegal, opposed the liberal conception of freedom of
the press. Nigerian journalists led the English-
speaking delegates in advocating the Western
libertarian press philosophy. Nigeria had been brought
up in a commercial system where free competition exists
among newspapers.

420. SALU, Adekunle. "Educational Broadcasting in
Modern Nigeria," E.B.U. Review, no. 95, 1966, pp. 25-
27.
This is one of the many articles written by
professionals in the industry on educational
broadcasting.

421. SALU, Adekunle. "Broadcasting, the Greatest Mass
Medium in Nigeria." E.B.U. Review, no. 103b, may 1967,
pp. 63-64.

From a very humble beginning in 1932, the Nigerian
Broadcasting Corporation has dramatically emerged as
the greatest medium of mass communication in the
country.

422. SCHRAMM, Wilbur et al. The New Media: Memo to
Educational Planners. paris: UNESCO, 1967.
This report is based on a research project financed
through a contract with the United States Agency for
International Development. It synthesizes case studies
gathered in three UNESCO-International Institute for
Educational Planning. The case studies include
projects in Algeria, Niger, Togo, Ivory Coast and
Nigeria.

423. SCHULTZ, Dagmar. "Broadcasting in Africa, With
Specific Emphasis on West Africa." M.A. thesis,
University of Michigan, 1965. Contains valuable
information on Nigerian broadcasting though author
looks at broadcasting in Africa.

424. SCHWARZ, F.A.O. Nigeria: The Tribes, the Nation
or the Race -- The politics of Independence. Cambridge:
MIT Press, 1965.
A discussion of Nigeria's political development, and
the role of newspapers in the movement for nationalism.

425. SELLERS, W. "Mobile Cinema Shows in Africa,"
Colonial Review, vol. 9, no. 1, 1955, pp. 13-14.
The author, a cinema technician for four years in
Nigeria, describes the technique of operating outdoor
mobile cinema shows on vans.

426. SENG, Michael P., & Gary T. Hunt, "The Press and
Politics in Nigeria: A Case Study of Developmental
Journalism," Boston College Third World Law Journal,
vol. 6, no. 2, 1966.
This paper's focus is on the role of the press in a
free society vis-a-vis government controlled or
developmental journalism. The example used is Nigeria
where the Buhari regime made serious efforts to
completely redefine the purpose of the press. Inherent
in the authors' discussion is the consideration of the
issue of whether or not Western models of a free press
should be imposed on developing countries. A brief
history of the press and its tradition of press freedom
is given.

427. SHAW, Trevor, & Grace Shaw. Through Ebony Eyes:
Evangelism Through Journalism in West Africa. London:
United Society for Christian Literature, Lutterworth
Press, 1956.

How and why did the <u>Christian Challenge</u>, a religious
magazine, start in Nigeria? The authors provide
insights to the beginning of the <u>Challenge</u> magazine
started by evangelists in Nigeria.

428. SHOBOWALE, Olalekan O. <u>The Professionalization
of Nigerian Media Staffers</u>. Ph.D dissertation,
University of Minnesota, 1984.
Examines the background and career characteristics of
Nigerian working journalists and the efficacy of some
generalized expectations about their promotion of
national development. The main findings are that
professional journalism in Nigeria is an area of
activity for the fairly educated, urban, young males
from upwardly mobile backgrounds. Two areas that need
to be reinforced are professional associations and
self-regulation.

429. SHOKUNBI, Fola M. "The Andrew Young Affair: A
Descriptive Evaluation of Newspaper Performance in
Nigeria, Israel, and the United States." M.S. thesis,
San Jose State University, 1980.
This study's aim is to find out if the editorial
positions of four newspapers -- the <u>Jerusalem Post</u> of
Israel, the <u>New York Times</u>, the <u>Atlanta Constitution</u> of
the United States and the <u>Daily Times</u> of Nigeria --
which in the past supported Andrew Jackson Young as the
U.S. ambassador to the United Nations, changed in the
aftermath of the controversy on Young's meeting with a
P.L.O. representative better known as the "Andrew Young
Affair." Only the <u>Daily Times</u> of Nigeria showed
evidence of reportorial bias after the incident.

430. SHORE, Larry. "Mass Media for Development: A
Reexamination of Access, Exposure, and Impact," In
Emile G. McAnany (Ed.), <u>Communications in The Rural
Third World: The Role of Information in Development</u>
(pp. 19-45). New York: Praeger Publishers, 1980.
This study examines the distribution and stratification
of mass media in rural areas in developing countries
with special focus on the composition of the audiences
for the various media and how the social stratification
of rural audiences affects issues of media access,
exposure, content understanding and utilization. A
case study on Nigeria shows that the stratification of
media exposure follows such factors as education and
economic resources. A mass media exposure model for
Nigeria is provided.

431. SKLAR, Richard L., & C.S. Whitaker, Jr.
"Nigeria," In James S. Coleman and Carl C. Roseberg,
Jr. (Eds.), <u>Political Parties and National Integration</u>

in Tropical Africa. Berkeley, California: University
of California Press, 1964.
This book contains analyses of politics and political
developments in African countries south of the Sahara.
Reference is made to the relationship between the West
African Pilot and the Zik Group of newspapers on one
hand and the NCNC political party on the other hand.
Information on the relationship between the Daily
Service and the Action Group (opposition group) party
is also provided.

432. SMITH, Jasper K. "The Press and Elite Values in
Ghana, 1962-70," Journalism Quarterly, vol. 49, no. 4,
1972, pp. 679-683.
Although this study's focus is on the Ghanaian press,
it contains part of an address by Herbert Unegbu
(editor of the West African Pilot -- one-time most
influential Nigerian newspaper) -- at the annual
assembly of the International Press Institute in 1965.

433. SMYTHE, Hugh H. "Problems of Public Opinion
Research in Africa," Gazette, vol. 10, no. 2, 1964, pp.
144-153.
An attempt to examine the nature and complexity of
public opinion research in Africa. Some of the
problems that could face scholars wishing to conduct
this form of mass communication research on the
continent are highlighted. Nigeria is mentioned in
this study, and its findings are applicable to the
country.

434. SOBOWALE, Idowu A. "Nigerian Newspapers'
Handling of Important National Issues: Ownership as an
Influence in News Coverage." M.S. thesis, Syracuse
University, 1976.
An investigation into the effect of newspaper ownership
on Nigerian press coverage of two important national
issues -- the Udoji Awards (the report of commission
set up to review salaries of government employees) and
the university student crisis of 1975. Six national
English-language dailies, three of them, government-
owned, are used for the study.

435. SOBOWALE, Idown A. Characteristics and
Professional Attitudes of Nigerian Journalists. Ph.D
dissertation, Syracuse University, 1978.
This study examines the characteristics and
professional attitudes of Nigerian journalists on their
jobs. Journalists in eight of the nineteen states are
surveyed. It is assumed that to understand the
professional journalist, it is necessary to understand
the socio-economic, psychological and organizational

factors as well as other constraints that motivate the individual journalist to behave the way he or she does. A casual model of professionalization among journalists is tested with data gathered in Nigeria. While the model tested does not find support among Nigerian journalists, a warning is offered that the model should not be abandoned.

436. SOKOMBA, Jonathan A. "Reception, Understanding and Use of Extension Publications by Extension Workers in Nigeria," M.S. thesis, University of Wisconsin, 1977.
Very little attention has been paid to the utilization of extension publications in the communication of agricultural information to Nigerian farmers. This study evaluates the extent to which such publications have been received and utilized by agricultural extension workers in Nigeria.

437. SOMMERLAD, Lloyd. The Press in Developing Countries. Sydney: Sydney University Press, 1966.
A description of the mass media in the developing countries. Focus is particularly made on the problems of mass media growth. Nigerian press is covered in this often-referenced book.

438. SONAIKE, Adefemi S. "Exploring Indicators of Public Opinion in Nigeria With Special Reference to the Letter to the Editor Column," Nigerian Journal of Economic and Social Studies, vol. 20, no. 1, 1978, pp. 37-53.
In this paper, `letters to the editor' are considered as indicators of public opinion in Nigeria. There is absence of formalized channels for determining public opinion in Nigeria. Letters to the editor appear to be the most promising alternative indicators of public opinion. Data from the Daily Times gathered in the study suggests that feedback to newspaper editors through `letters to the editor' has potentials as indicators of public opinion in Nigeria, and could provide policy makers an index of attitudes and opinions prevalent in their communities.

439. SONAIKE, Adefemi S. "Going Back to Basics: Some Ideas on the Future Direction of Third World Communication Research," Gazette, vol. 40, no. 2, 1987, pp. 79-99.
This study suggests some areas where future research studies on Third World Press may be directed. The author appears to have used Nigeria as a case study, and suggests the need for up to date studies on Nigerian media: number of radio and television sets,

circulation figures for the ten largest national and regional newspapers and the kinds of media most people rely upon for information in the country. Mention is also made of press freedom, ownership and national development.

440. SONUBI, O. "Trade Disputes in Nigeria, 1966-1971," Nigerian Journal of Economic and Social Studies, no. 15, 1973, pp. 221-237.
An analysis of trade disputes in Nigeria between 1966 and 1971 with special mention of how Decree No. 53 of 1967, Trade Dispute Decree, specially had the effect of restricting publication of news of trade disputes or industrial crises in newspapers.

441. SPAULDING, William E. Books in West Africa: Report and Recommendations. New York: Franklin Publications, Inc., 1963.
This report's main focus is on the general question of book publishing in West African countries, including Nigeria. The author believes that an African-European-American cooperation is one sure way to improving book publishing in West Africa. The report contains thirteen recommendations on how to improve book publishing in the region.

442. SPENCER-WALTERS, Tom J. Reconceptualizing Development Journalism: A Comparative Study of Four African Nations (Tanzania, Nigeria, Sierra Leone, Kenya). Ph.D. dissertation, University of Washington, 1987.
The study set out to examine African newspaper content as a series of problematic situations in order to formulate a theory of news as discrepancy. Four newspapers -- The Daily News (Tanzania), The Daily Mail (Sierra Leone), The Daily Nation (Kenya) and The Daily Times (Nigeria) -- were content-analyzed for the study. The main conclusion of the study is that news in the African context is perceived as a product of culture and therefore integrally operative within those cultural guidelines.

443. TAMUNO, T.N. Nigeria and the Elective Representation, 1923-1947. London: Heineman Educational Books, Ltd., 1966.
The author, one of Nigeria's well respected historians, provides valuable information on the role of the press in the politics of the colonial period of Nigerian journalism history. The book provides information on the cause and course of the enactment of the first press law as well as press and public reactions to the

law.   Editorial comments of some early newspapers on
various colonial government policies are provided.

444.   TAMONO, T.N.   The Evolution of the Nigerian
State: The Southern Phase, 1898-1914. New York:
Humanities Press Inc., 1972.
This book is concerned with the political development
of southern Nigeria until 1914, the year southern and
northern Nigeria were amalgamated. However, it
reflects a mirror-image account of the place of the
press in that process of development. In addition, it
describes the development of the Seditious Offences
Ordinance of 1909. The author notes that the
inaccurate translation of "sedition" as Temblekun
(civil war or conspiracy) in the Yoruba translation of
the ordinance, added more fuel to the fire of criticism
of the press law by the Central Native Council and the
public at large.

445.   TANJONG, Enoh.   Understanding National and
International Mass Media Use and Effects in a Third
World Setting: Evidence From Nigeria. Ph.D
dissertation, University of Wisconsin-Madison, 1986.
An investigation of the use and possible effects of
mass media in Nigeria, and the potential effects of
exposure to international media on opinions held of
foreign countries and the importance placed on various
world problems. The study concludes that urban
Nigerians use the radio somewhat more than either
television or newspapers. For international media use,
BBC is listened to by majority of urban Nigerians,
followed by VOA and Radio Moscow. Exposure to BBC is
found to be positively related to favorable audience
opinions of Great Britain, while VOA and Radio Moscow
exposure had no significant association with audience
opinions toward the U.S.A. and Soviet Union
respectively.

446.   TEDROS, Gabriel.   "Television in Africa,"
Gazette, vol. 8, 1962, pp. 189-191.
A description of the beginning of television in Africa,
where as of 1961 only three public television services
existed: the United Arab Republic (UAR), Nigeria and
Zimbabwe. Information on Nigerian television
transmitters, receivers and educational programming is
provided. The author's main thesis is that 50% of TV
program time be devoted to practical education and art.

447.   TOHOMDET, Obadiah S.D.   "The Role of the United
States in Nigerian Broadcasting." M.S. thesis, Iowa
State University, 1982.

Describes United State's influence on Nigerian broadcasting system. By the 1960's, the U.S. began broadcasting aid to Nigeria, using such private organizations like the Rockefeller Foundation and the Ford Foundation, providing funds, books, and broadcasting to schools. The U.S. influence came through the U.S.I.A., International Communication Agency (ICA), Agency for International Development (AID), American television networks and commercial Hollywood film companies.

448. TOPUZ, Hifzi. "News Agencies in Africa," Gazette, vol. 8, no. 1, 1962, pp. 48-51.
This article presents a panoramic view of the development of news agencies in African countries, including Nigeria where an information agency that precedes the News Agency of Nigeria (NAN) was established in 1961. The plan for the establishment of the information agency was ratified in July 1960.

449. TRABER, Michael. The Treatment of the Little Rock, Arkansas, School Integration Incident in the Daily Press of the Union of South Africa, West Nigeria and Ghana From September I to October 31, 1957. Ph.D dissertation, New York University, 1960.
The concern of this study is to identify and analyze the degree and focus of attention given to the little Rock, Arkansas, school integration incident in the daily press of South Africa, Western Nigeria and Ghana, from September I, to October 31, 1957. Four of the twenty-four dailies studied were from Western Nigeria. In the Nigerian papers, the incident is found to have gained substantially in significance in connection with the segregation incident at Dover, Delaware, involving the Ghanaian Finance Minister. The Nigerian papers are also found to express race consciousness which tended to identify the African-American with the African both in terminology and concern for the cause of the African-American.

450. TURNER, L.W., & F.A. W. Byron. Broadcasting Survey of British West African Colonies. London: Crown Agents, 1945.
Contains results of a survey of broadcasting in four former British West African colonies: Cambia, Ghana, Sierra Leone and Nigeria.

451. TURPEAN, Anne B. "The Government and the Newspaper of Nigeria." M.A. thesis, Howard University, 1962.
Author examines the relationship between the newspaper press and government in the pre-independence period.

An Annotated Bibliography

452. UCHE, Luke U. "The Politics of Nigeria's Radio
Broadcast Industry," Gazette, vol. 35, no. 1, 1985,
pp. 19-29.
This study examines the historical development of radio
broadcasting in Nigeria, and attempts to demonstrate
how Nigeria's political development has constantly
altered and influenced the structure of the
broadcasting system. The main conclusion is that like
Siamese Twins, broadcasting and politics in Nigeria are
inseparable; any surgical operation aimed at separation
that is not carefully carried out could lead to the
death of one, if not both.

453. UCHE, Luke U. "The Youth and Music Culture: A
Nigerian Case Study," Gazette, vol. 37, nos. 1-2,
1986.
A study of youth and music in Nigeria, part of ICYC
project. It reflects a critical and descriptive
analysis of how the inter-dependence and relationship
between music and FM-stereo format influences the music
orientation of the Nigerian youth. Rock, Disco, Reggae
and Calypso appeal to Nigerian youth the most. The
main conclusion is that Nigerian youth preference of
foreign music is fastly eroding their cultural root,
and they may be up as a people without a cultural base,
having courted foreign products at the expense of their
cultural pride.

454. UCHE, Luke U. The Mass Media Systems in Nigeria:
A Study in Structure, Management and Functional Roles
in Crisis Situations. Ph.D dissertation, The Ohio State
University, 1977.
This study integrates three research methodologies:
audience research analysis, historical analysis and
critical analysis to look into the structural and
management problems of mass media institutions in
Nigeria and their functional roles during some past
major national crises. One of the basic aims of the
study is to ascertain what opinion leaders in Nigeria
perceive to be the principal functions the mass media
perform in crisis situations and how they react to
mediated messages during such crisis situations.

455. UCHEGBU, Benjamin O. The Nature of Colonial
Anti-Nationalist Propaganda in British Africa: The Case
of Colonial Film Censorship in British Nigeria: 1945-
1948. Ph.D dissertation, New York University, 1978.
This study analyzes the censorship reports filed by the
colonial Board of Film Censors in Nigeria to determine
the criteria used in judging the films and the
relationship of the criteria to nationalists'
aspirations. The analysis reveals that the implicit

censorship criteria involved three central concerns:
the promotion of "law and order," the projection of
"white supremacy," and the projection of "Negro
inferiority."

456. UDOEYOP, N.J. "Scholarly Publishing In Nigeria,"
Scholarly Publishing, vol. 4, no. 1, 1972, pp. 51-60.
A description of the evolution of Nigerian publishing,
focussing particularly on the University of Ibadan
press. With higher education in Nigeria making
tremendous strides, the opportunities for scholarly
publishing are growing, but to date, British publishing
houses dominate the scene. This means that Nigerian
scholarly presses face ordinary monetary problems that
beset such organizations plus the disadvantageous
economic situation peculiar to developing countries.
Several of the publications of the University of Ibadan
press, including journals, are described.

457. UGBOAJAH, Frank O. "Developing Indigenous
Communication in Nigeria." Journal of Communication,
vol. 29, no. 4, 1979, pp. 40-45.
As a medium of mass communication, the radio has not
been productive in bringing about projected socio-
economic change in rural parts of Nigeria. Presently,
broadcasting is programmed to appeal to the tastes and
desires of the urban elite. The author suggests that
the key to creating a more indigenous style is to
recognize the essentially community-oriented nature of
African countries.

458. UGBOAJAH, Frank D. Communication of Development
Issues in the Nigerian Mass Media: A Sociological
Perspective. Ph.D dissertation, University of
Minnesota, 1975.
The attitude of key decision-makers in the Nigerian
mass media on four major issues of conflict in the
national development plan period, 1970-1974, and how
these issues were communicated in the mass media, is
the central focus of this study. Geographical location
rather than media ownership, among other factors, tends
to influence attitudes affecting the Nigerian
journalist's communication of conflict issues.

459. UGBOAJAH, Frank O. (Ed.), Mass Communication
Culture and Society in West Africa. Munich: Hans-Zell
Publisher, 1985.
A collection of twenty-six articles on several aspects
of mass media and mass communication in West Africa,
including Nigeria. Topics covered include: government-
press relations, press freedom and censorship, patterns
of ownership, academic and professional training,

diffusion of information and the New World Information Order. The primary objective of the book is to bring together for the first time a representative sample of some of the best articles and original research produced by West Africans over the last ten years, according to the author.

460. UGBOAJAH, Frank. Communication Policies in Nigeria. Paris: UNESCO, 1980.
Describes Nigeria's communication policies, and in addition, reflects on some of the press laws designed to check journalists. Those laws include contempt of court and obscenity laws.

461. UGBOAJAH, F., & I. Sobowale., "The Press in West Africa: A comparative Analysis of Mass Media Trends, In John A. Lent, (ed.), Case Studies of Mass Media in the Third World (pp. 133-152). Williamsburg, VA: Dept. of Anthropology, College of William and Mary, 1980.
In this paper the authors review mass media trends in Nigeria and the Cameroons, and pinpoint obstacles to their effective functioning in the aid of true socio-economic development. Government ownership of the media does not seem to influence the content of the media. There is self-censorship by many journalists.

462. UGWU, Godwin. "Managing Television in Developing Countries," Combroad, no. 49, 1980, pp. 13-17.
The author, Managing Director of Nigerian Television Authority (Zone C), draws on his experience to highlight some of the problems in using television for education, entertainment and socioeconomic development in the developing countries, including Nigeria.

463. UKPO, Etim J. Communication Technology and Strategies for Rural Development: The Case For Family Planning and Health Care in Nigeria. Ph.D dissertation, Wayne State University, 1974.
This study is another effort to examine the place of mass media in the success or failure of information diffusion on family planning and population control in Nigeria. The author recommends that traditional and modern media technologies should be used to increase the awareness of family planning programs in the country.

464. ULANSKY, Gene. Nnamdi Azikiwe and the Myth of America. Ph.D dissertation, University of California, Berkeley, 1980.
What was Dr. Azikiwe's myth of America? This study is another effort to document some of Azikiwe's journalistic contributions not only to Nigerian

nationalism and independence, but also to the black
race as a whole. The study looks at Azikiwe's myth of
America, through which he gave Africans a psychological
tool for competing equally with the West and for
asserting their role on the world stage. For many who
have heard much but known little about Dr. Azikiwe, the
founder of one-time Nigeria's most successful
newspaper, the _Pilot_, this study is one that can be
recommended.

465. UME-UWAGBO, Ebele N. "Politics and Ethnicity in
the Rise of Broadcasting in Nigeria, 1932-1962,"
Journalism Quarterly, vol. 56, no. 4, 1979, pp. 816-
821, 826.
Although broadcasting is a monopoly of the government,
the competition between broadcasting services run by
the states and federal broadcasters has allowed for
some diversity in programming and information. This
mixture of state-federal services evolved as a result
of the cultural and ethnic diversity which is reflected
in the distinctive characters of the regions of the
federation.

466. UME-UWAGBO, Ebele N. "Foreign News in Africa: A
Content Analytical Study on a Regional Basis," _Gazette_,
vol. 29, no. 1/2, 1982, pp. 41-56.
The study examines the patterns of foreign news flow in
Africa, by geographic region, and aims to find out the
extent to which African media reflect foreign norms,
especially western press norms, and the extent to which
African media promote national constituent regional and
inter-regional interests and aspirations. Nigeria is
one of the countries in the geographic groupings.

467. UME-UNAGBO, Ebele E. "Broadcasting in Nigeria:
Its Post-Independence Status," _Journalism Quarterly_,
vol. 61, no. 3, 1984, pp. 585-592.
Nigeria has two sets of broadcasting systems, one run
by the federal government, the other run by the states.
Despite the multiplicity of channels and program
choices, "grass root" programming and effective public
participation are absent. The post-independence period
is marked by the absence of clear objectives and
direction from federal and state governments. Sub-
standard equipment and program materials are other
problems that plague the system.

468. UME-UWAGBO, Ebele. "'Cock Crow at Dawn': A
Nigerian Experiment With Television Drama in
Development Communication," _Gazette_, vol. 37, no. 3,
1986, pp. 155-167.

This study examines the dramatic attributes of "Cock Crow At Dawn," an NTV program which combines conventional documentary and dramatic styles in motivating and instigating social change, particularly in ordering a modern approach to farming in Nigeria. The program has made a modest but important contribution toward agricultural revolution, and as a documentation in film-fiction, it is a television success story.

469.   UNEGBU, Herbert.   "Africa -- The Press in One Party State."   Paper delivered to the International Press Institute Assembly in London, May 25-27, 1965. The author, one-time editor of the West African Pilot, talks of the state of the press in a one party state with special reference to freedom of the press in Nigeria.

470.   UNESCO.   Statistics on Radio and Television 1950-1960. Paris: UNESCO, 1963.
Provides data on broadcasting in forty-seven African countries.   Program breakdown by music, news and twenty-three other themes are provided with more detailed breakdown for Morocco, Mozambique, Tunisia and Nigeria.

471.   UNESCO.   Meeting on the Introduction and Development of Television in Africa. Paris: UNESCO, 1964.
UNESCO report on a meeting held in Lagos September 21-29, 1964 concerning broadcasting needs in former British colonies in Africa, including Nigeria.

472.   UNESCO.   New Educational Media in Action: Case Studies For Planners. Paris: UNESCO, 1967.
A three-volume report on case studies of educational media in Africa.   The third volume focuses on three of such studies dealing with educational television in Nigeria.

473.   UNESCO.   Book Development in Africa: Problems and Perspectives. Paris: UNESCO, 1969.
Report of a conference of experts on problems and implications of book development in Africa with particular reference to what was, and should be the economic and social role of books and book publishing in African countries, including Nigeria.

474.   UNESCO.   Statistical Yearbook. Paris: UNESCO, 1984.
This reference book provides tables and information on several subjects about each country.   About Nigeria,

statistical data is provided on the number and
circulation of daily and non-daily newspapers,
newsprint production, imports and consumption, film and
cinema importation, radio and television broadcasting:
number of transmitters and transmitting power.

475. U.N. (United Nations). Statistical yearbook:
1983/1984. New York: United Nations, 1986.
This annual publication provides a comprehensive
compendium of the most important internationally
comparable data for the analysis of socio-economic
development at the world, regional and national levels.
About the press in Nigeria, information is provided on
newsprint consumption, number of daily and non-daily
newspapers, their circulation figures per one thousand
inhabitants and the number of radio and television
receivers.

476. USIA (United States Information Agency). "Basic
Attitudes and General Communication Habits of Four West
African Capitals." Washington, D.C.: USIA, July 1961.
This report by the research and reference service of
the United States Information Agency covers general
communication habits of audiences in Accra, Ghana;
Abidjan, Ivory coast; Dakar, Senegal and Lagos,
Nigeria.

477. USIA. "Foreign Radio Listening in Lagos,
Nigeria." Washington, D.C. USIA, October 1964.
A report of radio listening habits in Lagos, federal
capital of Nigeria.

478. USIA. "Mass Media Habits in West Africa."
Washington, D.C.: March 1966.
This report by the office of policy and research of the
United States Information Agency contains information
on mass communication habits of media audiences in West
Africa, including Nigeria.

479. USIA (United States Information Agency).
Communications Data Book For Africa. Washington, D.C.:
Government Printing Office, 1966.
This handbook provides useful information on
communication statistics for African countries more
than two decades ago. Nigeria, which is one of the
most developed countries in Africa had only 1.8 radio
receivers, 0.5 television receivers, .7 daily newspaper
copies and .1 cinema sets for every one thousand
persons by early 1960's. These figures do not meet the
UNESCO requirement of ten copies of daily newspapers,
five radio receivers, two television receivers and two
cinema sets for every one hundred inhabitants.

480. USORO, Ennutuk E. "An Analysis of Mass Media
Responsibility Toward Social and Political Growth in
Nigeria." M.S. thesis, Oklahoma State University,
1982.
An examination of the role concept for modernization
and place of mass media in development in Nigeria. The
study concludes that media practitioners are generally
more concerned about the Nigerian media industry than
serving the general public. Suggestions on how the
media can better serve the public are made.

481. UTOMI, Patrick. "Performance Under Constraints:
The Nigerian Press Under Military Rule." Gazette, vol.
28, no. 1, 1981, pp. 51-54.
The author considers some of the processes that were
involved in Army-press interaction in Nigeria during
the thirteen years (1966-1979) of military rule, and
the impact of such processes on the performance of the
press. The author concludes that while controls on the
press during the military rule may have been limited,
the extent of Nigerian press freedom during this era is
often overstated.

482. UTOMI, Patrick. "Ownership and the Development
Content of Nigerian Newspapers." M.A. thesis, Indiana
University, 1980.
How much influence does government ownership have, if
any, on the developmental content of newspapers in
Nigeria? This is the question this study set out to
answer. Other variables, rather than government
ownership, might be responsible for increased
developmental content in the two nation-wide
circulating dailies -- Daily Times and the Punch --
used for the study.

483. UTOMI, Patrick. "Historical-Philosophical
Foundations of Government Ownership of Newspapers in
Nigeria." Gazette, vol. 27, no. 1, 1981, pp. 69-72.
The historical-governmental characteristics of three
regions in Nigeria help explain the patterns of
government ownership of newspapers in Nigeria. The
Hausa-Fulani tradition in the north is one of
autocracy, due to the influence of Islam. The
constitutional monarchy of the Yorubas in the west led
to a system of give-and-take in government which
spawned a freer, more combative press. The east, had a
somewhat popular democracy which resulted in it being
the last area to have a government paper.

484. UYO, O'Kevbe A. Producers, Expressed
Participation in Program Decision Making and
Organizational Commitment in Nigerian Radio and

<u>Television Stations</u>. Ph.D dissertation, Syracuse
University, 1981.
This study investigates the relationship between
producers' expressed participation in program decision-
making, programming, and their organizational
commitment. It provides evidence which shows that
producers who expressed equilibrium have a stronger
organizational commitment than those who expressed
decisional deprivation.

485. VARIS, Tapio. "International Flow of Television
Programs." UNESCO Reports and Papers on Mass
Communication, no. 100, Paris, 1985.
A report on the international flow of television
programs and news in several countries, including six
African countries, among which is Nigeria. The report
summarizes the structure of programs in the six African
countries, and provides valuable information on
imported programs, total broadcast hours etc.
A casual comparison is made between broadcasting in
Nigeria and the other African countries.

486. WATERMAN, Christopher A. <u>Juju: The Historical
Development, Socio-Economic Organization, and
Communicative Functions of a West African Popular
Music</u>. Ph. D. dissertation, University of Illinois,
Urbana-Champaign, 1986.
Among other things, this study examines the social and
economic organization of juju music groups of Yoruba,
and analyzes the stylistic communication among juju
performers and patrons. The study points out that
African syncretic popular music may be usefully viewed
as systems of social and aesthetic communication, and
that the communicative role of musical style in urban
African contexts may strongly condition the development
trajectories of popular music.

487. WATTS, Ronald A. "African Journalism Institute,"
<u>Gazette</u>, vol. 14, no. 2, 1968, pp. 153-158.
A description of the nature, structure and programs of
the African Journalism Institute with special reference
to the International Federation of Journalists' (IFJ)
first attempt at training in Africa which took place in
1964 at Ibadan. Twenty-eight journalists from Sierra
Leone and Nigeria attended that training which served
as a guide for drawing up African Journalism Institute
program.

488. WAUTHIER, Claude. "PANA: The Voice of Africa,"
<u>Africa Report</u>, March-April, 1987, pp. 65-67.
This article describes the birth and role of the Pan-
African News Agency which has the Nigerian News Agency

as one of its members, and Lagos, as one of the five regional headquarters for its news pools. A casual reference is made to Nigerian press freedom. According to the author, Nigeria has managed to retain a range of newspapers of different opinions, although at a costly price. But almost everywhere else in Africa, news agencies, television, radio and newspapers are strictly government-controlled.

489. WEDDELL, E.G. "Broadcasting in the Developing Commonwealth," Combroad, no. 46, 1980, pp. 14-19.
A review of statistical and documentary data concerning broadcasting in ninety-one developing countries. Special focus is made on eleven countries, among them, Nigeria. Some of the areas covered include program content and educational broadcasting.

490. WEDDELL, E.G., & M.J. Pilsworth. "The Role of Broadcasting in National Development: Nigerian Case." Manchester, Department of Adult Education, University of Manchester.
This study uses Nigeria to examine the role of broadcasting in national development.

491. Western Nigeria Radio Services. Television in the New Nigeria. Ibadan: Western Nigeria Broadcasting Corporation, 1972.
A thirty-six-page compilation of papers celebrating "Television Week," a period during which Western Nigerian Broadcasting Service (WNBS) locally produced programs.

492. WESTLEY, David. The Oral Tradition and the Beginnings of Hausa Fiction. Ph.D. dissertation, The University of Wisconsin, Madison, 1986.
This study examines the nature of the Hausa oral tradition and assesses its influence on the development of written texts in Hausa. The study also assesses the effects of literacy on the development of narrative pattern in the oral tradition. The findings indicate that though the Hausa oral tradition provided inspiration for early Hausa fiction, it was a distinct medium of communication with its own oral conventions. Thus it provided an inadequate model for the development of written fiction in Hausa.

493. WHEATLEY, Ronald B. "An Exploratory Analysis of the Objects of Trust and Threat in the Political News of the Nigerian Popular Press." M.A. thesis, University of Washington, 1969.
In this research, three Nigerian newspapers - the West African Pilot, the Daily Times and the Daily Express

are used to examine the extent to which tribal attributes served as objects of internal trust and threat in the political news of the Nigerian popular press. The data reveals that there was very little evidence of tribal attributes serving as objects in the political news of the newspapers surveyed.

494. WHITEMAN, Kaye. "Nigeria's War: History Takes Over." Venture, no. 24, 1972, pp. 26-29. This article reviews some of the publications on the Nigerian Civil War. It concludes that the mine of first hand information has hardly been touched.

495. WILCOX, Dennis L. The Press in Black Africa: Philosophy and Control. Ph.D dissertation, University of Missouri - Columbia, 1974. This dissertation is a descriptive, comparative study of press-government relationships in the thirty-four nations of independent Black Africa South of the Sahara, including Nigeria. It discusses press restraints and ownership patterns of mass media in these countries. The study gives some background on Nigerian press, and shows how Nigeria weighs on a press freedom scale against other African countries.

496. WILCOX, Dennis L. Mass Media in Black Africa: Philosophy and Control. New York: Praeger 1975. A descriptive survey of government-press relationships in independent black Africa defined as those thirty-four nations south of the Sahara with black majority governments. The author systematically analyzes formalized press controls exerted by governments in order to find a pattern of evolving press philosophies and to show the function and role of the press. Nigerian press is well covered in this book.

497. WILCOX, Dennis L. "Press Controls in Sub-Sahara Africa," In J. L. Curry and J. R. Dassin (Eds.), Press Controls Around the World (pp. 209-232). New York: Praeger publishers, 1982. A review of press controls in thirty-eight independent nations in Africa, including Nigeria. Special focus is made on media ownership and the measures adopted by various governments to control the press. Nigeria is one of the countries with pluralistic media ownership, and diversity of viewpoints in the press. Other areas covered include: broadcasting, film, newsprint allocation and licensing.

498. WILKINSON, J.F. "The BBC and Africa." African Affairs vol. 71, no. 283, 1972, pp. 176-185.

An analysis of the role of the British Broadcasting
Corporation (BBC), and the development of broadcasting
in Africa. Special focus is made on Nigerian radio in
the 1950's. Despite some problems and pressures,
Nigeria has a strong team of professional broadcasters
who are determined to develop their services in the
national interest.

499. WILLIAMS, David. "Power in Restraint: Nigeria's
Press Prepares for October," IPI Report, vol. 28, no.
6, 1979, pp. 6-7.
This article looks at the Nigerian press in the wake of
the return to a democratically elected government,
following thirteen consecutive years of military rule.
Mention is made of the influence of the earlier
newspapers, including the West African Pilot, in
politics. The main point made is that the return to
civilian rule will give newspapers a new lease of life.

500. World Press: Newspapers and News Agencies. New
York: UNESCO and the UNESCO Publications Center, 1964.
A booklet containing information on the press
throughout the world. It describes newspapers and news
agency facilities in nearly two hundred countries,
including Nigeria. There were twenty-four dailies,
seventeen in English and six in bilingual editions by
1964 in Nigeria. It provides some background on
Nigerian press.

501. YOUNG-HARRY, Sunday. "The Effectiveness and
Evaluation of Educational Broadcasting in Nigeria,"
Combroad, no. 41, 1978, pp. 47-48.
A reflection on the ten objectives of the Nigerian
Broadcasting Corporation's educational service. The
major conclusion is that effective and successful
educational broadcasting requires cooperation from all
involved: educational agencies, schools, teachers,
program producers, broadcasting stations and
government.

Index

The numbers in the index refer to entry numbers, not page numbers.

Abuja: TV program 43
Access to government information 69
Accreditation of journalism programs: Nigeria & U.S.A.
    compared 374
Achebe, Chinua 119, 237
Action Group 431
Adamu, Haroun 91
Adult television & education 19, 122, 190, 312
Advertisements 191, 263, 371, 385
Africa 10, 14, 25, 61, 76, 131, 210, 470
Africa: Book publishing 244, 473
Africa: Commercial radio/ television broadcasting 120,
    131, 146, 154, 423, 498
Africa: Communication networks 242
Africa: Communication policy & population growth 409
Africa: Development journalism 184, 332
Africa: Freedom of the press, speech & assembly 50,
    232, 251, 267, 418, 495-7
Africa: Introduction and development of television 148,
    446, 471
Africa: Mass communication research sources 247-8, 337
Africa: Public opinion research 433
Africa: Television program production & exchange 306
<u>African Affairs</u> 267, 498
African-American actors in U.S. film industry 142
African-Americans 4, 415
African Council on Communication Development 10

African development 10, 114
African journalism history 245
African Journalism Institute 487
African news agencies 23, 173, 448, 500
African Press 14, 23, 29-32, 35, 61, 67, 114, 145, 155,
    164, 175, 188, 191, 208, 232, 240, 245, 247, 268,
    274, 418, 470, 495-7
African Report 179, 180, 250, 309, 402, 488
African schools of journalism (a list of) 239
African writers 130
Africscope 35
Agence France Presse 173, 231
Agricultural extension publications 436
Aikhomo, Augustus 107
Ajasa, Kitoyi 269
Ajasco: Indigenous medium of advertisement 263
Alagoa, Ambrose 57
Allegations of government corruption 63
The Amakiri (Minere) Affair 54-5, 57-8
Anambra Broadcasting Service 372
Anambra Television 122
Anglo-African 139
Apartheid: How Nigerian Press views it 64
Arson & vandalism in the media 351, 354
Asaju, Michael 118
Ascroft, Joseph 255
Asian Broadcasting Union Newsletter 317
Associated Press 173, 231
Association of Advertising Practitioners of Nigeria:
    Conflict with NPAN 364
Association of Nigerian Authors: Reaction to Newswatch
    ban 107
The Atlanta Constitution: Coverage of the "Andrew Young
    Affair" 429
Authoritarianism & the press 2, 238, 241, 245
Awolowo: Views on Press freedom & democracy 50
Azikiwe 71, 164
Azikiwe: Chain of newspapers 164, 266, 431
Azikiwe: Criticism of Nigerian Press 355
Azikiwe: Speech on newspaper regulation 138
Azikiwe: Speech on the role of NBC 138

Babangida & human rights 86
Babangida & the media 12, 83, 86-7, 100, 112, 180, 363,
    365
Babangida: Maiden broadcast 112
Bako, George 45-6
BBC 8, 102-4, 142, 445
BBC & the development of broadcasting in Africa 498
BBC: Coverage of students' unrest in Nigeria 102
BBC: Interviews with Junaid Mohammed 103-4
The Beatles 416
Bibliographical essay on Nigerian Press 337

Bibliography of African broadcasting: An annotated guide 248
A Bibliography of major publications on Africa 167, 247-8
A Bibliography of theses and dissertations in broadcasting: 1920-1973 275
Black Victorians 130
Boigny, Houphouet 238
Book censorship 99
Book distribution 27, 182
Books for the developing countries: Asia, Africa 230
Book publishing & problems 183, 230, 243-4, 286, 412, 441, 456, 473
Book publishing in Sierra Leone 244
Book publishing in West Africa 244, 441
Boston College Third World Law Journal 426
Bright-Davis, James 382
British liberalism & the development of Nigerian Press 4
British press and the "Dikko Affair" 307
Broadcast history 1, 6, 16, 48, 124-5, 151-2, 169, 170, 181, 197, 199, 202, 221, 227, 233, 262, 270, 273, 276-7, 280, 284-5, 293-4, 305, 386, 393-4, 403, 417, 452
Broadcast news content 231
Broadcast programming & production 122, 131, 178, 215-6, 229, 280, 293
Broadcasting & democracy 124, 140
Broadcasting & national development 1, 19, 26, 43, 149, 228, 249, 270, 279, 314, 366, 395, 457, 468, 490
Broadcasting & television in West Africa 205
Broadcasting Company of Northern Nigeria 181
Broadcasting: Frequency allocation 141
Broadcasting hours 215
Broadcasting in Africa 246-9, 280, 423
Broadcasting in Africa: A continental survey of radio and television 246, 280
Broadcasting in Nigeria 293
Broadcasting in Sierra Leone 233-4, 450
Broadcasting in the Third World: Promise and performance 270
Broadcasting in West Africa (the development of) 233
Broadcasting industry: Restructured & centralized 361
Broadcasting: Problems & obstacles 135, 148, 154, 170, 198, 215-6, 226, 279, 285, 377, 394, 462, 467
Broadcasting: Satellite 62, 90
Broadcasting: Staff training 280
Broadcasting survey of British West African colonies 450
Buhari & propaganda 186
Buhari (military government) & the press 75, 77-8, 83, 92, 108, 121, 144, 180, 253-4, 300, 338-41, 343-4, 360-1, 396, 426

Burma 27

Cameroonian press 461
Censorship 2, 12-3, 22, 34-5, 78, 83, 90-2, 95, 98-9,
     101, 105-7, 144, 159, 200, 210, 283, 301, 337,
     353, 397, 399, 440, 455, 459, 461
The Christian Challenge 427
Cinema attendance 329
Cock Crow at Dawn 468
Colonial Review 425
Communication policy 460
Communication research in the Third World: Future
     directions 439
Communication yearbook 335, 367, 370
Communications data book for Africa 479
Concentration of press ownership 321
Constitutional law of the Republic of Nigeria 324
Constitutional provisions on free press 179, 204
Contempt of court 84

Daily Express 415, 493
Daily Graphic (Ghana) & Daily Times (Nigeria):
     Comparison on press freedom 322
Daily Mail (Sierra Leone) 442
Daily Mirror 30
Daily Nation (Kenya) 23, 442
Daily News (Tanzania) 442
Daily Service 155, 431
Daily Sketch 64, 331
Daily Times 17, 20, 23, 64, 66, 69, 100, 109, 111, 160,
     164, 251, 322, 331, 335-6, 369, 371, 385, 415,
     429, 438, 442, 482, 493
Decree no. 2 of 1984 103, 338-41
Decree no. 4 of 1984 77, 82, 92, 96-7, 104, 121, 144,
     180, 300, 338-41, 343-4, 360, 396, 398
Decree no. 4 of 1984 (repeal of) 83, 86, 112, 338, 362
Decree no. 11 of 1976: Comparison with Decree no. 4 of
     1984 396
Decree no. 53 of 1967 440
The Democrat 81
Deportation of foreign correspondents 105
Detention of journalists 12, 35, 77-8, 91-6, 99, 101,
     103, 105, 253-4, 264, 298, 300, 338, 351, 356, 360
Developing countries 5, 15, 27, 148, 171, 177, 218,
     230, 430, 437, 462, 489
Developing countries: Book publishing 244
Developing countries: Broadcasting 270
Developing countries: Role of the communicator 211
Developing countries: Role of the media 60, 216, 287
Developing countries: Role of the university press 128
Developing countries: Satellite broadcasting 62, 207
Developmental communication 260, 334-6
Developmental journalism 187, 426, 442

116

Diffusion of information 11, 129, 171, 176, 223, 249,
    255, 271-2, 379, 409, 436, 459, 463
"Dikko Affair": It's reportage in Nigerian & British
    press 307
Doctoral dissertations (on Africa) 113

E.B.U. Review 48-9, 181, 221-2, 279, 294, 420-1
Economic Community of West African States 21
Economic hardship on the press 79-80
The Economist 34
Editor & Publisher 232
Editorial contents 16, 17, 250, 274, 369, 370
Educational broadcasting 5, 18, 24, 62, 125, 127, 135,
    152, 189-90, 222, 224, 270, 278, 280, 347, 420,
    446-7, 462, 472, 489, 501
EKPU, Ray 84
Ekwelie, Sylvanus 10
Ekwensi, Cyprain 237
Enahoro, Peter 251
Ethics & codes of conduct 51, 68, 76, 146, 265, 327,
    390, 428
Europa Yearbook 213
The evolution of the Nigerian state: The Southern phase
    1898-1914 444
External radio service 40, 229, 280
Eyutchae, Zrydz 251
Ezenta, Eze 67

Fawehinmi, Gani 89
Federal military government & international public
    relations 177
Federal Ministry of Communications 42
Federal Radio Corporation of Nigeria (FRCN) 36-7, 40,
    45, 372
FRCN: Executive appointments 46-7
FRCN: Objectives 226
FRCN: Role in arts & culture 395
FRCN: Role in national & international communication 45
Film (cinema) industry 9, 142, 224, 303, 320, 329, 366,
    425, 453, 474-5, 479, 497
Financial Times 111
First television in Africa 125, 136, 189, 199
Five Elections in Africa 295
Folk (traditional) media 133-4, 149, 223, 249, 263,
    457, 463, 492
Foreign broadcasts (ban of) 90, 102-4, 109
Foreign correspondents in Nigeria 70, 98, 104-5, 283,
    402
Foreign news 3, 8, 15, 23, 111, 173, 331, 369-70, 410-
    1, 466, 485
Free Press of Ghana 109
Freedom of political expression (in U.S.A. India &
    Nigeria) 215

INDEX

The Fugitive offender: The study of a political
      prisoner 209
The Fundamental & Adult Education 347

The Gambia: Development of broadcasting 233
The Gambian broadcasting 450
The Gambian press: Its role in nationalism 311
Gaskiya Ta Fi Kwabo: Its Contents 250
Gazette 29, 30-1, 149, 185-7, 193-5, 198, 200, 239,
      251, 327, 331, 336-7, 369, 372, 385, 388, 399,
      409, 416, 433, 439, 446, 448, 452-3, 466, 468,
      481, 483, 487
Ghana: Book publishing 244
Ghana: The NRC & the media 241
Ghana: Television program production & exchange 306
Ghanaian & Nigerian press coverages of immigrant
      expulsions 109
Ghanaian broadcasting 109, 233-4, 450
Ghanaian press 4, 109, 201, 241, 385, 432, 449
Ghanaian Press: Its role in nationalism 311
Giwa, Dele 85-6, 88-9, 153, 406
Government media 8-9, 16-7, 69, 118, 159, 169, 174,
      192, 195, 259, 261, 310, 399, 434, 451, 482-3
Government media: Economic problems 236
Government posters 310
Government Publications Review 310
Government reaction to BBC coverage of students' unrest
      102
Government reaction to Dele Giwa's death 85
Gowon, Yakuba 54, 56, 59, 186
Grassroots broadcasting 36, 227, 467
The Guardian (London) 111
The Guardian (Nigeria) 77, 96, 109, 111, 369-70
Guyana 287

Halilu, Adamu 142
Hausa 28, 492
Hausa (written) fiction 492
History of the Nigerian Broadcasting Corporation 285
Hong Kong 287
Huxley, Elspeth 50

Ibrahim, Mohammed 47
Ibrahim, Rufai 96
Ifudu, Vera 292
Ikoku, Sam 99
Immigrant expulsions (Ghanaian & Nigerian press
      coverage of) 109
Index on Censorship 91-107, 121, 175
India 214
Indiana University communications project in Nigeria
      405
Indigenous publishers 183-243

INTELSAT 25, 33, 207
Intercultural communication 184, 242
International Communication and Youth Culture
    Consortium 416, 453
International communication: Media, channels, functions
    224
International Federation of Journalists 115, 487
International flow of television programs 485
The International Law of Communications 207
International news flow 3, 8, 15, 23, 109, 111, 173,
    231, 246, 256, 331, 369-70, 410-1, 449, 466, 485
International Perspectives on News 203, 345
Interpersonal communication 133-4, 149, 184, 242, 325,
    366
IPI General Assembly in Lagos 64-6, 432
IPI: Reaction to imprisonment of journalists 77
IPI Report 22, 50-90, 153, 159, 268, 288, 298, 300,
    349-65, 396-7, 413, 418-9, 499
IPI training course on Lagos 52
Irabor, Nduka 97
Israeli press: Coverage of the "Andrew Young Affair"
    429

Jackson, John Payne 269
Jackson, Thomas Horatio 269
Jakande, Lateef 60, 81, 356, 465, 467
Jakande: Criticism of Nigerian press 355
Jerusalem Post 429
Jose, Babatunde 66
Journal of African History 383
Journal of African Studies 290
Journal of Broadcasting 146, 148, 247
Journal of Commonwealth Political Studies 158, 235
Journal of Communication 457
Journal of Developing Areas 289
Journalism education 10, 52, 67, 115, 126, 185, 239,
    241, 283, 327, 374, 389, 391, 401, 418, 459, 487
Journalism Educator 374
Journalism Monographs 184
Journalism Quarterly 32, 114, 134, 199, 204, 218-20,
    241, 302, 313, 320-2, 368, 371, 375, 401, 411, 432
Journalism training on the job 71, 131, 459
Journalistic practice & performance 79, 83, 118, 156,
    160, 187, 237, 259, 312, 389-92, 418, 428
The Journalist's World 115, 136
Judiciary & the press 34, 57-8, 84, 88-9, 96, 204, 298,
    356, 358-9, 388, 392
Juju music 486

Kenya 23
Kenya: Concentration of press ownership 321
Kenyan press & pre-independence elections 295
Kitchen, Helen 155

Kuti: Release from jail 101

The Lagos Standard 382
Le Monde 111
Leopold, Senghor 22
Liberian broadcasting 234, 306
Licensing 497
A Life of Azikiwe 266
Low cost receiver 348
Lugard, Frederick 382

Macauley, Herbert 269
Maduka, Vincent 42, 44
Magazine publishing 413, 427
Making the News 231
Mass Communication Culture and Society in West Africa
     459
Mass Communication in Africa 312
Mass media development (in Africa) 114, 422
Mass media exposure & preferences 184, 260, 329, 330,
     367, 430, 445, 476-8
Mass media research on West Africa: Current status &
     future directions 194
Media & presidential system of government 38
Media Asia 329
Media guide for Nigeria, Ghana, Liberia & Sierra Leone
     234
Media ownership 9, 16-7, 187, 192-3, 195, 283, 380,
     390, 439, 459, 483
Media uses & gratifications 28, 260
Mexico 27
Military rule 2, 17, 60, 108, 144, 172
Military government & the press 2, 12-3, 17, 22, 35,
     54-60, 69, 86-7, 90-2, 95, 99, 106-8, 121, 144,
     172, 180, 200, 253-4, 264, 267, 283, 338-41, 343-
     4, 378, 381
The Mirror 111
Missionaries & literacy activities 130
Mobile broadcasting 39, 393
Mobile cinema 425
Modibbo, Dahiru 46
Mohammed, Junaid 103
Movie theatres 234
Mozambiquan press: Comparison with Nigerian press
     freedom 175
Multi-lingual broadcasting 26, 228
Music 416, 453, 486

NAEB Journal 125-7, 154
NAEB Review 278
National Concord 95, 109, 369-71
National news agencies 15, 173
New Nigerian 17, 20, 64, 69, 109, 331, 334-6, 369

New World Information Order 15, 256, 372, 459
New York Times 111, 429
News Agency of Nigeria 15, 173, 179, 213, 349, 448, 500
News agents 138
News imbalance 3, 15, 369-70, 372, 410-1
Newspaper Act (of 1964): Its roots 296, 338, 342
Newspaper & the law 291
Newspaper circulation 30, 172, 235, 288, 320-1, 474-5,
    479
Newspaper contents 16-7, 23, 32, 250, 256, 259, 369-71,
    410-1, 482
Newspaper houses: Their names & addresses 147, 315,
    318-9, 384
Newspaper Ordinance (of 1903) 338, 343, 346, 384
Newspaper proprietors Association of Nigeria 54, 353-4,
    364
Newspapers 8, 20, 139, 145, 150, 155, 160, 164, 168,
    175, 187, 195, 213, 235, 274, 288, 311, 318, 352,
    384, 400
Newspapers in Belgian, British & French colonies 30
Newsprint: Problems, production & consumption 116, 474-
    5, 497
Newsprint shortage 61, 80, 352
Newswatch 12, 84-9, 106-7, 406, 372, 459
Newswatch ban & public reactions 106, 107
Newsweek 105
Nigeria & the elective representation, 1923-1947 443
Nigeria Magazine 130, 191, 376, 382
Nigerian & Ivorien newspapers compared 238
Nigerian authors 119
Nigerian Broadcasting Corporation (NBC) 18, 36, 49,
    124, 151, 221-2, 270, 285, 305, 316-7, 421, 501
NBC: Its objectives 501
NBC: Ten years of service 316
NCNC Party 341
Nigerian Chronicle 331
Nigerian editors 69, 168
The Nigerian federal elections of 1959: Politics and
    administration in a developing political system
    407
Nigerian government & politics: Prelude to the
    revolution 298
Nigerian government & politics under military rule
    1966-1979 264
Nigerian Guild of Editors 51, 54, 69, 145, 353-4
Nigerian Information Bank 25
Nigerian Institute of Journalism 53, 118
Nigerian Institute of Public Relations 408
Nigerian Journal of Economic & Social Studies 243, 438,
    440
Nigerian journalism: Problems 118, 418
Nigerian journalists 3, 13, 15, 20, 30, 69, 130, 139,
    173, 187, 286, 304, 428, 435

Nigerian journalists: Their reaction to Decree No. 4
    (of 1984) 300
Nigerian newspaper: Their problems 158, 172, 235, 352,
    400, 418, 437, 454, 461
Nigerian novelists 119, 205, 237, 286
Nigerian Observer 54, 58
Nigerian Opinion 8, 189, 236, 366
Nigerian Outlook 415
Nigerian periodicals & newspapers, 1950-1955 318
Nigerian periodicals: Their addresses 147, 213
The Nigerian Pioneer 382
Nigerian press & WWII 250
Nigerian press: Biases in international news coverage
    369-70
Nigerian press: Changes in technical quality sales &
    advertisements 191
Nigerian Press Council 179, 327, 349-50, 365
Nigerian Press Council Decree 169
Nigerian press coverage of African-Americans 415
Nigerian Press Law 206
Nigerian Press Organization 68, 353
Nigerian press view on apartheid 64
Nigerian Security Organization 96
Nigerian Statesman 369
Nigerian Television: Its problems 198
Nigerian Television Authority (NTA) 37, 39, 41-2, 43-4,
    198, 215
NTA & Vera Ifudu 292
NTA appointments & dismissals of managers 41-2, 44
NTA Calabar 37
NTA: Cultural form 122
NTA Enugu 122
NTA: Lapses & abuses 198
NTA: Staff reassignments 43
NTA: Staff training 126
Nigerian Trade Journal 116
Nigerian Tribune 22, 93
Nigerian Union of Journalists (NUJ) 54, 96, 107, 110,
    145, 353, 359
NUJ: Its code of conduct 265
NUJ: Reaction to Newswatch ban 12, 107
Nigerian Yearbook 319
Nigerian Youth & music interpretations 416
Nnamdi Azikiwe & the Myth of America 464
Northern Nigerian Television (sound broadcasting
    services) 48, 181
Nwankwo-Ifejika (Publishing) Company 182

Obituary advertisements 371, 385
The "Oilgate" scandal & the press 156
Ojukwu & propaganda 186, 326
Onitsha market literature 182
Operation Feed the Nation & the press 11

Opinion leaders & opinion leadership 132, 454
Organization of Islamic Conference (criticism of) 101

Pamphlets 182, 379
Pan African Journal 328
Pan African News Agency 488
Partisan press 117, 299, 355, 376, 407, 434
Perspectives of empire 123
The Philippines 242
Photojournalism 20
Pioneer journalists 139, 225, 381, 384
Police-press relations 63
Political parties and national integration in tropical
    Africa 431
Politicians & greed 289
Politicians & regulation of broadcasting 328
Preface to modern Nigeria 282
Press & elections 8, 295, 407
Press & elections in Sierra Leone 295
Press & industrial relations 196
Press & Nigeria-Biafra war 402
Press & political partisanship 117
Press & politics 8, 16, 38, 64-6, 68, 71, 109-11, 113,
    117, 123-4, 137, 137, 140, 143, 150, 157-8, 161-5,
    167-8, 201, 209, 217, 240, 250, 257-8, 261, 266,
    269, 282, 295-6, 299, 307, 311-2, 337, 346, 373,
    376, 384, 424, 426, 443-4, 452, 465, 493, 499
Press & politics in Nigeria 1880-1937, 384
Press & public reactions to Newspaper Ordinance 443
Press & rural/national developments 1, 4, 11, 19, 25-6,
    31, 38, 43, 129, 135, 146, 149, 158, 171, 178-9,
    184, 187, 203, 216, 220, 223, 228, 249, 272, 279,
    287, 299, 309, 333, 345, 366, 403, 430, 436, 439,
    457-8, 463, 480, 490
Press coverage of foreign affairs 109, 110-1, 307, 410
Press coverage of Little Rock Arkansas school
    integration incident, 449
Press coverage of South African state of emergency 111
Press coverage of the "Andrew Young Affair" 429
Press coverage of "Udoji awards" 434
Press freedom 2, 7, 9, 12-3, 16-7, 22, 30, 34-5, 50,
    54-60, 63, 66, 70, 72-8, 82-3, 86-7, 91-7, 99-108,
    112, 121, 138, 145, 156, 158-9, 169, 174-5, 179-
    80, 200, 204, 206, 208, 210, 214, 217, 219, 232,
    240-1, 244, 251-4, 264, 266, 281, 283, 298, 302,
    313, 320, 322, 337-41, 343-4, 346, 351, 362-3,
    375, 378, 383, 387-8, 396-9, 418-9, 426, 439-40,
    451, 459-60, 469, 481, 488, 495-7
Press history 1, 6, 14, 16, 29-32, 71, 81, 88, 110,
    139, 143, 145, 155, 157, 159-61, 168-9, 182, 191,
    193, 206, 225, 240, 274, 282-3, 288, 296, 311,
    319, 337, 342-3, 346, 373, 381, 384, 387-8, 400-1,
    403, 426-7, 443-4, 448

The Press in Africa 274
The Press in developing countries 437
Press laws 29, 31, 77, 82, 84, 91-2, 96, 103, 108, 121,
    161, 169, 206, 217, 257, 283, 291, 296, 308, 324,
    342, 357, 375, 384, 387-8, 390, 396, 404, 443-4,
    460
Press ombudsmanship 327
Press opposition of British colonial policies 123, 137,
    157, 162-5, 168, 201, 209, 217, 257-8, 266, 269,
    282, 311, 346, 373, 384, 423, 443-4
Press reaction to Decree No. 4 (of 1984) 398
Press role in Sierra Leone independence 331
Press role in W.W.I 382
Press support for British colonial policy (W.W.II) 250
Prime time programming 122
Printing industry 243
Professionalism 29-30, 51, 61, 68, 79, 118-9, 173, 236,
    241, 264-5, 301-2, 304, 327, 392, 428, 435
Propaganda 326, 455
Propaganda techniques in Africa 186
Provincial newspapers 160, 175, 179, 213, 250, 500
Public opinion indicators (in Nigeria) 438
Public opinion research in Africa: Its problems 433
Public reactions to British colonial policies 123
Public reactions to creation of Press Council 350
Public reactions to Giwa's death 85
Public reactions to Seditious Offences Ordinance 444
Public service broadcasting 5, 18
Public television in UAR 446
Publications on the Nigerian Civil War 494
Publicity channels 147, 223, 310, 319
The Punch 91, 95, 331, 482
Pye project 39

Quill 156

Radio broadcasting 1, 5-6, 9, 16, 18, 26, 31, 36, 38,
    40, 45, 120, 131, 140-1, 153, 166, 170, 179, 181,
    189, 191, 202, 205, 213, 221-2, 226-9, 231, 233-4,
    246, 248-9, 270, 275-7, 279-81, 284-5, 293-4, 305,
    314, 316-7, 328, 347-8, 361, 372, 395, 403, 417,
    420-1, 423, 447, 450, 452, 465, 467, 470-1, 474-5,
    479, 484, 489-90, 497-8
Radio broadcasting & foreign policy 40
Radio executives & bribery scandal 358
Radio forum experiments 347
Radio: Future developments & prospects 140-1, 154, 170,
    189, 285
Radio in Africa: Problems & prospects 154
Radio Kaduna 181
Radio listenership 135, 234, 281
Radio Moscow 445
Radio news 372

Radio Nigeria 1, 6, 9, 18, 26, 31, 140-1
Radio: Number of sets per 100 persons 320, 474-5
Radio programme production: A manual for training 131
Radio: Staff training 280
Radio station burning 351
Radio stations: Their names & addresses 147
Rand Daily Mail 23
Regional newspapers 160, 169, 175, 250
The release of journalists & political detainees 82,
    94-5, 97, 104, 112
Religious broadcasting 246
Religious press 160, 169, 195, 427
Retrenchment of journalists 79
Role of radio broadcasting (in southern Nigeria) 273
Role of the NBC 317
Role of the press under military government 236
Rural Africana 133
Rural press 224

Satellite 25, 33, 62, 206
Satellite broadcasting 62, 90, 207
Satellite dishes 90
Scholarly Publishing 12, 183, 456
School broadcasting 18, 24, 222
Secondary school students & journalism career 368
Seditious Offences Ordinance 444
Senegal 22
Shehu Shagari & propaganda 186
Shehu Shagari: His government & the press 34, 42, 70,
    72, 204, 353, 357
Short-wave broadcasting 40
Sierra Leone: Book publishing 244
Sierra Leone: Development of broadcasting 233-4, 450
Sierra Leone: Television program production & exchange
    306
Sierra Leonian press (contents) 442
Sierra Leonian press & pre-independence elections 295
Sierra Leonian press: Its role in independence 311
Singapore 287
Society of Nigerian authors 119
Sociology & Social Research 242
Solarin, Tai 93
Soldiers & Power: The development performance of the
    Nigerian military regime 378
Sound broadcasting: Its evolution 227
Sources in African mass communication research 247-8,
    337
The Sources of Nigerian law 404
South Africa 23, 111, 242, 449
South African journalists & IPI assembly in Lagos 64-6
Southern Nigerian Defender 209
Soyinka, Wole: His early writings 290
Soyinka, Wole: His political expressions & imprisonment

414
Students & media preference 369
Student (campus) newspaper 185
Sunday Satellite 95
Survey of the technical development of the Nigerian
    Broadcasting Corporation 305

Talking drums 249
Tanzanian Press 245, 442
Taxation without representation 123
Telecommunications 21, 25, 33, 207, 403
Television advertisements 234, 263
Television & national development 43, 146, 149, 178,
    216, 279, 366, 386, 462
Television broadcasting 9, 19, 24, 31, 37, 39, 43, 48,
    62, 118, 120, 122, 124-7, 136, 146, 151-2, 169-70,
    181, 190-1, 197-8, 202, 205, 213, 215-6, 229, 231,
    233-4, 246, 248, 262-3, 279, 284, 297, 306, 313,
    328, 361, 377, 380, 386, 393-4, 403, 417, 446,
    462, 465, 467-8, 470, 472, 474-5, 479, 484, 490-1
Television: First in Africa 125, 136, 189, 199
Television houses: Their names & addresses 147
Television: Number of sets per 100 persons 320, 474-5
Television program production & exchange in West Africa
    306
Temblekun 444
Third World communication research: Future directions
    439
Thompson, Tunde & Nduka Irabor: Their release from
    prison 360
Times of Ghana 385
Times of Nigeria 382
Torture of journalists 35, 54, 57, 72-3, 77, 85, 153,
    200, 253-4, 264, 267, 300, 338
Totula, Amos 237
Trade disputes decree 440
Trade publications 160

Udoji awards: How the press covered it 434
UNESCO 114, 131, 148, 332, 422
USAID 127
United Arab Republic: Public television 446
United Christian Association: Poster distribution 101
United States 10, 214, 242, 429, 445
United States International Cooperation Administration
    & the development of mass media in Nigeria 405
U. S. press coverage of the "Andrew Young Affair" 429
United States' role in the development of Nigerian
    broadcasting 447
U.S. News & World Report 50
University of Ibadan (Press): Publications 456
University of Nigeria: Its communication department
    185, 239

University press 128

<u>Venture</u> 494
Vernacular newspapers 160, 250, 500
Visnews 231
Voice of Nigeria 40

<u>Washington Post</u> 111
West Africa 108-10, 117-8, 142, 145, 225, 233-4, 292,
     307, 398
West Africa: Book publishing 244, 441
West Africa journalists 115
<u>West Africa Pilot</u> 29, 71, 137, 155, 164, 196, 209, 225,
     251, 258, 266, 410-1, 431-2, 493, 499
West African Press 2, 4, 6, 14, 21, 30-1, 137, 194,
     205, 261, 288, 311, 383-4, 419, 423, 450, 459-60
<u>West African Review</u> 276
Western Nigerian Television: WNTV/WNBS 125, 136, 189,
     197, 199, 491
<u>Wilson Quarterly</u> 286
Women: Group communication 133
Women in the media 20, 304, 368
<u>World Press Encyclopedia</u> 283
<u>World Press Freedom Review</u> 73-4, 78, 83, 86
<u>World radio television handbook</u> 229
World War II & the development of radio 273

About the Compiler

CHRIS WOLUMATI OGBONDAH is an assistant professor of Journalism at the University of Northern Iowa. He has been news editor and senior producer at the Nigerian television, Ibadan as well as assistant editor of the *Nigerian Tide* in Port Harcourt. Author of five journal articles on international communication, Ogbondah's research interests are in comparative mass media systems.